The Practice of Qualitative Data Analysis

Research Examples Using MAXQDA

The Practice of Qualitative Data Analysis

Research Examples Using MAXQDA

Edited by

Michael C. Gizzi

Stefan Rädiker

ISBN: 978-3-948768-10-2 (paperback)
ISBN: 978-3-948768-05-8 (eBook PDF, identical page numbers as paperback edition)
https://doi.org/10.36192/978-3-948768058

© MAXQDA Press, Berlin 2021, 1st edition

MAXQDA Press is a division of VERBI Software. Consult. Sozialforschung. GmbH
Invalidenstr. 74, 10557 Berlin, Germany, info@maxqda-press.com, www.maxqda-press.com

Printed by Books on Demand, Norderstedt, Germany

Contents

Table of MAXQDA Key Features Covered

Use the following table to identify chapters in which your MAXQDA function of interest is described in the research example. The table is ordered by the MAXQDA main menu.

MAXQDA feature	Book chapters (chapter starts on page)
Home	
Teamwork Export/Import	Ch. 10 (p. 169)
Import	
Import Documents from Excel Spreadsheet	Ch. 10 (p. 169)
Import Focus Group Transcripts	Ch. 5 (p. 89)
Codes	
Color coding (highlight coding)	Ch. 1 (p. 17)
Comments on coded segments	Ch. 10 (p. 169)
Creative Coding	Ch. 1 (p. 17)
Smart Coding Tool	Ch. 1 (p. 17)
	Ch. 4 (p. 71)
	Ch. 6 (p. 107)
Memos	
Memos	Ch. 1 (p. 17)
	Ch. 6 (p. 107)
	Ch. 7 (p. 121)
	Ch. 8 (p. 135)
	Ch. 9 (p. 149)
	Ch. 10 (p. 169)
Variables	
Document Variables	Ch. 3 (p. 55)
	Ch. 4 (p. 71)
Import Document Variables	Ch. 6 (p. 107)
Speaker Variables	Ch. 5 (p. 89)
Analysis	
Lexical Search	Ch. 4 (p. 71)
	Ch. 5 (p. 89)
	Ch. 9 (p. 149)

Introduction

Michael C. Gizzi, Stefan Rädiker

MAXQDA is a powerful tool for qualitative and mixed methods research. The research community that uses MAXQDA spans the globe. This book brings together examples of the diverse types of research that MAXQDA can be used for. While researchers have access to a detailed user manual, multiple books that provide in-depth background about the software's functionality, and an active research blog, this book fills in a missing gap—providing case studies with concise real-world examples from different disciplines and using different methods of how MAXQDA is used in practice.

The book illustrates more than 28 MAXQDA features and showcases how MAXQDA can be effectively used. Each case study provides a brief overview of the research topic being explored, the methodological approach, and a detailed description of how MAXQDA was used to conduct the research. The case studies focus on the usage of MAXQDA, and not the substantive research outcomes, and they answer a variety of practical questions for the reader, such as how the coding system was developed, how coded documents were analyzed, what tools were used, and how those tools informed the results.

Each chapter is intended to be used by researchers as a resource when approaching new projects. The book was inspired by the excellent research posters that have been presented at the MAXQDA International Conference in Berlin from 2017 to 2020 (conference.maxqda.com), as well as the numerous research blog posts on the MAXQDA website (maxqda.com/blog). The examples do not replace detailed user manuals or textbooks but provide the researcher with concrete examples that they can draw insights from in crafting their own research.

The book covers different methodologies, data types, and tools, including thematic analysis, qualitative content analysis, ethnography, and grounded theory, process-generated historical research, typology building, and more. The book is not comprehensive in covering every qualitative method used by scholars, nor is it intended to be a text to replace many of the books that give an overview of and describe several research methods (e.g., Creswell & Poth, 2018; Flick, 2014). This book, instead, is meant to provide real-world examples from research in a variety of disciplines and approaches, that are conducted almost entirely with MAXQDA.

Example-based learning

We approached this book out of a strong belief in the power of example-based learning. MAXQDA provides tools to conduct a qualitative analysis, and the user manual and other works, such as Kuckartz and Rädiker's *Analyzing Qualitative Data with MAXQDA* (2019) provide in-depth guidance about specific functions, but this book does something unique. It offers the reader insights into actual research projects, providing examples that can serve to inspire the researcher. We were inspired ourselves by similar learning by example books, such as a text on SPSS (Morgan et al., 2006) that provided instructions on using statistical tools but included real-world examples and explanations of how to interpret results. *The Practice of Qualitative Data Analysis* isn't quite the same, as our focus is less on how to interpret analyses but more about the ways you can use software to conduct specific tasks in qualitative analysis. In this context, we would be remiss not to mention Nicholas Woolf and Christina Silver's *Qualitative Analysis Using MAXQDA: The Five Level QDA Method* (2018), which includes two case studies of how their five-level approach to qualitative analysis can be used in practice: Christian Schmieder's illustration of a thematic analysis evaluating an education program was particularly valuable for one of us (Michael) and served as a spark for providing better learning opportunities for showcasing the power of MAXQDA. It is perhaps no surprise that we invited Christian and his colleagues to contribute a chapter for this book.

In their review of example-based learning, van Gog and Rummel (2010) suggest that for novice learners, "instruction that relies more heavily on studying worked examples, than on problem solving is more effective for learning, as well as more efficient in that better learning outcomes are often reached with less investment of time and effort" (p. 156). We believe that an example-based book like *The Practice of Qualitative Data Analysis* is not only effective for novices but for researchers of all levels, from the undergraduate user of MAXQDA conducting their first research project to doctoral students working on their dissertation to researchers who have been working with qualitative data for years. Case studies of how others have completed a project, with a clear description of what they did, can serve to inspire the reader in ways that a textbook often cannot do.

The examples in this book come from many disciplines, such as education, health sciences, history, sociology and social sciences, political science, criminal justice, and public policy and cover several topics. One of the great advantages of example-based learning is that you can learn from every chapter, regardless of what discipline, topic, or method it deals with. You might not think a study of historical legal documents from 400 years ago might be relevant to your own work, but the methods and visualizations that Andreas Müller uses in chapter 3 are applicable to many studies. Likewise, you might not be an educational specialist, but you can learn from the ways Natalie Santos, Vera Monteiro, and

Lourdes Mata combined focus groups of students with interviews of teachers in chapter 2 and the ways they used MAXQDA's tools to inform their analysis.

Of course, everyone needs to learn on their own, and there is no better way to learn MAXQDA than to use it and to learn from your mistakes. You will develop your own best practices, but this book will help shorten the learning curve, and you can potentially avoid pitfalls that slow down research or make it less efficient. To that end, each chapter ends with a section titled "lessons learned" in which the authors provide their own advice about what they learned from their experiences, and you can draw from that.

Overview of research examples

The Practice of Qualitative Data Analysis includes ten chapters that provide you with a wide range of approaches and experiences, from different disciplines, using a variety of methods. There is some overlap in chapters in terms of how they use specific tools, but we are not trying to present case studies of just unique tools, but instead want the reader to see the contributor's chapter as a fully explained example of they used MAXQDA to conduct their research. You will also find different uses of the same tools, like the Summary Grid and Table. For example, Michael Gizzi and Alena Harm illustrate in chapter 4 how they used the Summary Grid to reduce coded segments to more concise summaries, while Aikokul Maksutova used the Summary Grid in an entirely different way to create in-depth summaries of documents (chapter 8).

As the Table of Key Features (pp. 7–8) shows, the ten research examples cover a lot of tools in MAXQDA. The book intentionally does not include every tool in MAXQDA or every method you can use the software for—this would be an impossible task—, but we offer a wide selection from the diverse world of qualitative data analysis:

Chapter 1. Using MAXQDA in Ethnographic Research: An Example with Coding, Analyzing, and Writing

Danielle Jacques provides an example of ethnographic research on public transportation in Senegal using a grounded theory and thematic analysis approach. The chapter shows how she developed a multi-level coding system, illustrating the usage of color coding (with the pen highlighter) to do a descriptive coding cycle, followed by a cycle in which she added thematic codes. The Smart Coding Tool and the Creative Coding tool were used to organize the resulting code system, and the Code Relations Browser helped to identify patterns and relationships.

Chapter 2. Using MAXQDA in Qualitative Content Analysis: An Example Comparing Single-Person and Focus Group Interviews

Natalie Santos, Vera Monteiro, and *Lourdes Mata* offer a case study of a qualitative content analysis in the field of education, comparing single-person interviews (of teachers) with student focus groups provide. They provide a detailed description of their use of MAXQDA's visual tools, including MAXMaps, the Document Portrait, Code Matrix Browser, and Code Relations Browser. Finally, they explain the usage of the Summary Grid and the Summary Tables to organize the findings and draw conclusions.

Chapter 3. Using MAXQDA's Visual Tools: An Example with Historical Legal Documents

Andreas Müller demonstrates how MAXQDA can be used with process-generated data, like court records, media reports, and other materials, but from the perspective of a historian looking at court records from the 16th and 17th centuries. He uses the Compare Groups function, the Code Matrix Browser, and the Code Relations Browser to identify differences between documents, relations between codes, and changes of subjects over time. The chapter provides an example of how the Document Comparison Chart can be used in an analysis to examine the internal structure of documents by using meaningful code colors.

Chapter 4. Using MAXQDA from Literature Review to Analyzing Coded Data: Following a Systematic Process in Student Research

Michael Gizzi and *Alena Harm* provide a case study in the field of criminal justice of how MAXQDA can be used by student (and other) researchers in a systematic way from the creation of a literature review through coding analyzed data. The chapter draws on step-wise learning to provide a structured approach to conducting a research project and discusses the usage of numerous tools for paraphrasing, memo writing, restructuring codes, as well as an easy-to-replicate process for analyzing coded data.

Chapter 5. Using MAXQDA for Analyzing Focus Groups: An Example from Healthcare Research

Matthew Loxton provides a detailed explanation of how he uses focus group data in the field of health sciences in chapter 5. He shows how focus group transcripts are imported into MAXQDA and the ways that the user can fix errors from transcripts. The analysis of focus group transcripts is illustrated using a variety of tools such as the Word Cloud, Keyword-in-context, and Document Portrait, and how to prepare writing of the report using the Summary Grid.

Chapter 6. Using MAXQDA for Analyzing Documents: An Example of Prioritization Research Design in Urban Development

Temur Gugushvili and *Gvantsa Salukvadze* showcase how they analyzed documents to identify and prioritize relevant topics in the field of urban development. After applying thematic codes in combination with evaluative codes, they used the Smart Coding Tool to check the coding integrity, while Code Configurations allowed them to explore code co-occurrences. The visual tools MAXMaps and Document Portrait were utilized to visualize the relations and proportions of identified topics. By awarding points depending on assigned codes, scores for the importance of each topic were calculated.

Chapter 7. Using MAXQDA for Identifying Frames in Discourse Analysis: Coding and Evaluating Presidential Speeches and Media Samples

Betsy Leimbigler provides a research example from political science in the area of American presidential politics and media coverage in chapter 7. She used discourse analysis to explore the "frames" used by American presidents surrounding health care reform. Beginning with a deductive set of six broad codes derived from the literature, she added several inductive sub-codes to explore the frames in greater depth. Leimbigler illustrates how memo writing was key to her analysis, particularly for summarizing hundreds of documents. While Code Frequency charts illustrated the usage of frames, the Code Relations Browser helped to explore connections between the frames.

Chapter 8. Using MAXQDA's Summary Features: Developing Social Types in Migrant Integration Studies

Aikokul Maksutova demonstrates how MAXQDA's summary functions were used in a sociological study of the integration of labor migrants from three countries in Central Asia in chapter 8. She explains how the interview data were analyzed in several steps, increasing the level of abstraction at each step, finally leading to a typology with social types: First, the Summary Grid was used to summarize thematic highlights for each interview. Second, the summaries per topic were compiled in Summary Tables for each investigated country, and were, third, consolidated into "summaries of summaries" which formed the basis of the final typology.

Chapter 9. Using MAXQDA for Bibliographic Documentary Analysis: Combining Automatic and Manual Procedures Within a Literature Review

Antoni Casasempere-Satorres and *Marisa Vercher-Ferrándiz* present an approach for rapidly but thoroughly conducting a literature review, the so-called Bibliographic Documentary Analysis. This kind of analysis combines automatic and manual procedures: Among other things, they show how they use Lexical Search and Word Combinations to identify relevant terms and concepts, and how they code and paraphrase appropriate search hits. The juxtaposition of paraphrases in the Paraphrase Matrix, as well as a complementary code system that reflects the structure of the final report, support the writing of the literature review.

Chapter 10. Using MAXQDA in Teams and Work Groups: An example from Institutional Evaluation and Organizational Data Analysis

Christian Schmieder, Joel Drevlow, and *Josset Gauley* share how they work and communicate together as a team to analyze a constantly growing dataset with MAXQDA. The demonstration project involves several persons divided into four different roles (lead, manager, analysis team, and data users). They present their workflows to distribute MAXQDA projects among team members and how they use the Teamwork Export and Import features to bring it all together in one master file again. Among other tools, Comments on coded segments and Paraphrases are used to develop suitable coding schemes.

Acknowledgments

We began talking about the idea of a book of case studies at the 2019 MAXQDA International Conference (MQIC), after being impressed by the diverse posters that were presented at the annual conference. A year later we moved to make the idea a reality and began work. The pandemic eliminated our plans to meet for a week on the project in Berlin in June 2020, but we quickly adapted to virtual meeting tools and began a year-long collaboration which has resulted in the book before you.

We are especially grateful to the incredibly talented individuals who responded to our invitation to participate in this project. We pushed hard for short-deadlines, and each chapter went through numerous revisions as we sought to provide consistency in the structure and style but still let the individual author's own ideas and intellectual process for using MAXQDA come through. We also are particularly grateful to those who are writing in a second or third language in this book. While our editing has attempted to provide a coherent American English feel, we are so pleased by what the final product is. Any errors remain ours and not our contributors.

We also want to give our thanks to Dr. Udo Kuckartz, the founder and creator of MAXQDA, for his support and encouragement in the development of this book. Thanks are also due to the staff at VERBI and MAXQDA Press in Berlin, including Anne Kuckartz, Isabel Kuckartz, and Aikokul Maksutova. Elizabeth Jost and Sarah Schneider were incredibly helpful in the early stage of the book, as we were seeking to identify individuals to participate in the book.

Michael Gizzi wants to also thank his wife Julie for her support during this year of "work from home," in encouraging me to develop the book. As has been true for years, William

Wilkerson and Ethan Boldt have served as sounding boards, even though neither are MAXQDA users. He also especially wants to thank his co-editor, Stefan Rädiker, for agreeing to take a chance on this book and pushing it forward over this past year.

Stefan Rädiker thanks his wife Marina for her always clear view of things and bringing-up helpful questions, not only while he was working for this book project. Special thanks also go to his co-editor, Michael Gizzi, for the extremely productive exchange that made this exciting book project possible. It was a great pleasure to work together on the book and to have the possibility to learn so much in the process.

Bibliography

Creswell, J. W., & Poth, C. N. (2018). *Qualitative inquiry and research design: Choosing among five approaches* (4. ed.). Sage.

Flick, U. (Ed.). (2014). *The SAGE handbook of qualitative data analysis*. Sage.

Kuckartz, U., & Rädiker, S. (2019). *Analyzing qualitative data with MAXQDA: Text, audio, and video*. Springer Nature Switzerland. https://doi.org/10.1007/978-3-030-15671-8

Morgan, G. A., Leech, N. L., Gloeckner, G. W., & Barrett, K. C. (2007). *SPSS for introductory statistics: Use and interpretation* (3rd ed.). Erlbaum.

van Gog, T., & Rummel, N. (2010). Example-based learning: Integrating cognitive and social-cognitive research perspectives. *Educational Psychology Review*, 22(2), 155–174. https://doi.org/10.1007/s10648-010-9134-7

Woolf, N. H., & Silver, C. (2018). *Qualitative analysis using MAXQDA: The five-level QDA method*. Routledge.

Using MAXQDA in Ethnographic Research:
An Example with Coding, Analyzing, and Writing

Danielle N. Jacques

Abstract

Using the example of my 2018 Master's thesis on public transportation in Senegal, I show how MAXQDA may be used to code and analyze ethnographic data. Field observations and semi-structured interviews were conducted to investigate the "*car rapide*" mini bus system as a space for cultural production and participation while situating it within a larger political discourse on modernity. Coding was conducted in three cycles using a grounded theory approach in conjunction with descriptive and thematic coding. Highlighter pen codes were utilized to perform a descriptive coding cycle in which each type of bus was catalogued. Thematic codes were superimposed on top of the descriptive highlight codes. The resulting code system was organized using the Creative Coding Tool, and patterns and relationships were identified using the Code Relations Browser. Complex Coding Queries were conducted to add context and color to the relationships identified in the Code Relations Browser. The thesis that resulted from this work provided an ethnographic account of the soon-to-be-retired *car rapide* ecosystem while also situating the debate over its retirement in political and historical contexts.

Key MAXQDA features covered

- ✓ Color coding (highlight coding)
- ✓ Smart Coding Tool
- ✓ Creative Coding Tool
- ✓ Memos
- ✓ Code Relations Browser
- ✓ Complex Coding Query

1 Introduction to the research questions

My research is a mini-ethnography of public transportation in Dakar, Senegal, and specifically of the *car rapide* (CR) mini bus. The CR is a ubiquitous form of public transportation that has been in circulation in Dakar since 1947, when the vehicles were first imported from France to transport merchandise. Adorned with colorful paintings that represent traditional and contemporary Senegalese culture and used by individuals of all socioeconomic backgrounds, the CR is one of the most instantly recognizable symbols of Senegal today.

Despite their cultural significance, however, the *car rapide*'s reign over the streets of Dakar may soon be coming to an end as a result of the targeted initiatives of the Emerging Senegal Plan (ESP). The ESP is a developmental framework that aims to achieve middle-income status in Senegal by 2035 through a series of structural transformations of the economy, the promotion of human capital, and good governance.

My research sought to understand the *car rapide* as a space for cultural production and participation, while also situating it within a larger political discourse on development and modernity. While the central goal of my research was to provide an ethnographic account of the soon-to-be-retired *car rapide* "ecosystem"—everything from the way in which one rides the CR, how its routes and fare systems work, and how it compares to other forms of public transit in the city—it also asked the following questions: How do middle class Dakarois feel about the loss of a cultural icon in the name of "modernity?" How do they envision the future of public transportation in Dakar?

2   Data collection and methodological approach

This study is the result of qualitative research conducted in Dakar in December 2017, during which I performed a participant observation of the *car rapide* and other bus systems in the city. I boarded buses at their point of origin in different neighborhoods, rode them to the end of the line, and then boarded another bus to make the return trip. I also observed people at bus stops and recorded the frequency and availability of the multiple bus systems that operate simultaneously in Dakar. When possible, I engaged strangers in short, interview-like conversations that centered around their opinion of the CR's cultural significance and looming retirement.

I also conducted 15 semi-structured interviews of 60 minutes in length. The sample included 12 men and 3 women from middle to upper class backgrounds. All interlocutors had extensive experience with the CR as their main form of transportation around the city. The interviews provided color and depth to the ethnographic observations I gathered and probed deeply on the respondents' attitudes toward the CR's retirement and the modernization of public transit in Dakar as a whole.

Field notes and interview transcripts were analyzed in MAXQDA using a grounded theory approach as suggested by Saldaña (2016) and Birks and Mills (2012). In essence, grounded theory "involves meticulous analytic attention by applying specific types of codes to data through a series of cumulative coding cycles that ultimately lead to the development of a theory" (Saldaña, 2016, p. 55). In other words, grounded theory seeks to find emergent themes in the data rather than impose a predetermined theory or lens upon them.

Coding was conducted in three cycles. First, descriptive coding was applied to each transcript in which general topics of conversation were identified. Next, the transcripts were revisited using initial coding, in which tentative codes were applied to the data based on emerging themes, ideas, and theories. In vivo coding, the act of creating codes using direct quotes and phrases from informants, was also applied at this stage. Finally, a third cycle of coding was applied in which the initial codes were refined and further analyzed.

Utilizing a grounded theory lens enabled me to uncover themes that I would not have found if I had been approaching the data from a purely developmental framework, as is often the case when it comes to public transportation. Literature on public transportation in developing countries often adopts an urban planning lens and stresses the need to reduce congestion and motorization. Dakar in particular has been the focus of many transportation studies due to its status as a pilot city for many of the World Bank's transportation infrastructure projects. Although my data certainly spoke to these themes, coding inductively from a grounded theory perspective allowed me to uncover a larger political discourse about what it means to be "modern" in Dakar.

3   First cycle coding

Although my fieldwork focused on the *car rapide,* it quickly became apparent that it is impossible to discuss one form of transportation in Dakar without making references to the other bus systems that operate simultaneously. In that regard, I decided to use descriptive coding as my first cycle coding strategy. Unique codes were created for each mode of transportation in Dakar and were applied on a sentence-by-sentence basis. For example, a sentence referring to the "Tata" minibus system was coded with "TATA," and so on. In the event that a sentence discussed two or more types of transportation, I applied the respective codes concurrently to the same segment of text, resulting in overlapping coded segments.

While descriptive coding is most commonly achieved in MAXQDA using regular codes, I relied on the highlighter pen tool to conduct my descriptive coding (**Highlight coding** is available in the toolbar of the Document Browser window by clicking on the colored pen icons). Color is a powerful analysis tool in MAXQDA, and this is especially true for the highlighter pens when used for descriptive coding; in addition to being able to glean the topic of the transcript without reading the text, color-coding my transcripts according to the bus(es) being discussed allowed me to visualize the ways in which my informants saw them as inextricably linked. Fig. 1 illustrates this phenomenon; because each bus type has its own color, I can quickly see that this respondent has referenced 3 different buses, often focusing on one bus briefly before switching subjects to another in his response to a single question.

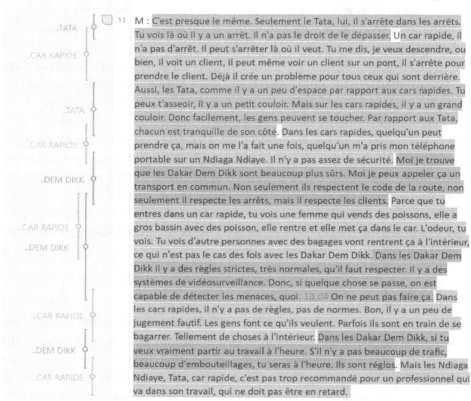

Fig. 1: Descriptive codes applied to the text using the highlighter tool, allowing the researcher to visualize shifts in the topic of conversation

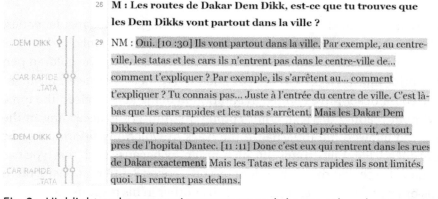

Fig. 2: Highlight codes are semi-transparent and change color when two or more colors are applied to the same segment of text. Used descriptively, they can help visually identify when two or more topics of conversation overlap

Furthermore, the semi-transparent nature of the highlighter pens allowed me to not only visualize shifts in conversation, but to also take note when two or more buses were being directly referenced or compared together. Take, for example, Fig. 2, where you can clearly see that the respondent referenced the *car rapide* (blue) and *Tata* (pink) buses in the same sentence, changing the paragraph's color to a new purple, while comparing both to the *Dem Dikk* bus (green).

Descriptive highlight codes were renamed directly in the Code System so that the name of each code was no longer the name of the respective color but instead matched the type of bus being defined; in that regard, "Blue" became "CAR RAPIDE," "Pink" became "TATA," and so on.

By descriptively coding each mode of public transit in my first cycle, I laid the groundwork for a more complex analysis in later phases, as I could then leverage tools such as the Code Relations Browser. Because subsequent coding cycles involved the application of thematic codes on top of these descriptive codes, further analysis would enable me to identify, compare, and contrast the lived experiences on each type of bus.

4   Second and third cycle coding

Once the transcripts had been fully descriptively coded with highlight codes, I revisited each text and coded the data using an initial coding approach. Initial coding "creates a starting point to provide the researcher analytic leads for further exploration" and results in a list of "proposed codes… [that are] tentative and provisional" (Saldaña, 2016, p. 115) and that may need further exploration or refinement. Initial coding works particularly well as a coding strategy for ethnographic data, as the codes created may be descriptive, theoretical, or conceptual in nature based on the type of data and the unique viewpoint of the researcher.

In this cycle, I created a large number of tentative codes based on emerging themes, theories, and ideas as I worked through my data. New codes were applied primarily by highlighting segments of text within the Document Browser window and manually creating a new code. However, with the advent of MAXQDA 2020, initial coding may be more easily achieved through the Open Coding Mode, which allows the researcher to quickly create large numbers of new codes within the text using fewer mouse clicks and dialog boxes (this mode is switched on by clicking on the icon **Open Coding Mode** in the toolbar of the Document Browser window).

Many of the codes created during the second coding cycle may also be considered descriptive in nature; because creating an ethnography of passenger experiences on the *car rapide* was central to my research, I coded for topical notions such as "routes," "time tables," "hours of operation," and "waiting for bus," just to name a few. I also created descriptive codes for the various actors involved in operating the bus, such as the drivers and *apprenti* (young men in charge of collecting fares).

Other codes created in this cycle were more thematic in nature and captured the larger political arguments made by my interlocutors surrounding the modernization of public transit in Dakar. Thus, while I coded for different aspects of waiting for, boarding, and riding the buses in Dakar, I also coded more abstract themes, such as the responsibility of the State to its citizens, respect for others, and *teranga* (hospitality).

The descriptive highlight codes created in the previous cycle were turned off for the duration of the second and third coding cycles. Codes, including highlight codes, can be toggled on and off by right-clicking in the coding strip on the left-hand side of the Document Browser window (Fig. 3). Hiding codes through this tool removes them from the display in the Document Browser without deleting them from the Code System. In this way, codes can be hidden and recalled, allowing the researcher to "declutter" the Document Browser view and focus on one or multiple codes, either for aesthetic or analytical reasons.

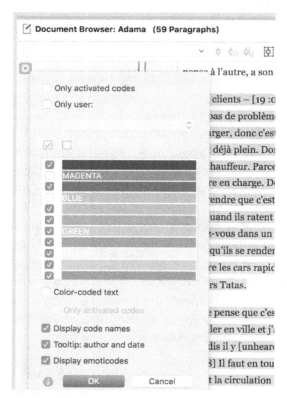

Fig. 3:   Clicking on the gear wheel icon or right-clicking in the coding stripe area on the left-hand side of the Document Browser allows the researcher to toggle the view of certain codes without deleting them from the code system. This tool may be leveraged for analytical or aesthetic reasons, such as to focus on just a few codes or to "declutter" the view

In vivo codes were also applied at this stage using the **Code in Vivo** icon in the toolbar of the Document Browser. In vivo codes use respondents' own words or phrases to capture "participants' words as representative of a broader concept in the data" (Birks & Mills 2015, p. 90). Kuckartz (2014) notes that in vivo codes "enable us to access the participant's observations directly, without obstructing them by the theories we develop" (p. 23). I created in vivo codes when a respondent said something that felt particularly striking or profound, or that underlined the ways in which they thought about public transportation and modernity in Dakar. In this way, nearly all of my in vivo codes encapsulated my respondents' political arguments for and against modernity, as well as their attitudes toward the government's ability to deliver on its promises of development.

Because in vivo codes are inserted into the Code System window as a top-level code, I organized them manually by creating a new code called "In Vivo Codes" and by moving all in vivo codes, each containing one coded segment, as sub-codes of this category (Fig. 4).

In Vivo Codes	0
Ca ne reste pas avec les Senegalais.	1
Comme ça se passe en Afrique, maintenant ça continue.	1
C'est ça, l'Afrique et malheureusement on est obligé de l'accep	1
Dakar est en plein évolution	2
Il faut pas refuser le développement.	1
Il voulait créer des histoires.	1
Ils doivent disparaitre.	1
Je pense que c'est de l'utopie.	1
La politique d'indiscipline	1
Le bon sens est la chose du monde la mieux partagée.	1
Mais c'est le sous-développement qui l'explique, eh	1
Mais c'est pas suffisant.	1
On est né, on voit les cars rapides, on a grandi, on voit les c	1
On ne veut pas changer. Ça fait partie aussi de notre culture.	1
On pense qu'on est bien quoi, un produit fini, alors qu'il y a	1
Prendre un car rapide c'est perdre du temps	1
Un véritable casse-tête.	1
Une conscience citoyenne faible est à l'origine de ces faits	1
c'est sur la route qu'on voit qu'il n'y a pas de tolérance	1
c'est un processus qui est toujours en cours, mais on peut dire	1
c'est africain, c'est typique	1
en Afrique les gens ont tendance de faire les choses que la loi	1
ici en Afrique les gens ne respectent pas les lois et c'est dom	1
il y aura une révolution, c'est sûr	1
le Sénégal ne reste pas les bras croisés	1
l'état du Sénégal ne peut pas, ne réfléchit pas en termes préve	1
l'état il n'a pas une politique de prévention	1
ça joue un rôle primordial à l'économie de notre pays	1
éradiquer cette fléau concernant le transport en commun	1

Fig. 4:   In vivo codes, each containing one coded segment, are sub-codes of a top-level category called "In Vivo Codes" for organizational purposes

Similarly, I created a code using the Gold Star emoticon and renamed it "Great Quotes." As I read through my transcripts, I coded sentences or passages that were particularly good at illustrating certain points as "Great Quotes." Sometimes but not always overlapping with the in vivo codes, this category allowed me to collect passages of text that would later serve as a repository of quotes to use when writing my thesis.

Once all transcripts had been initially coded in the second cycle, I revisited each transcript for an iterative third cycle in which I worked to apply new and existing codes to the data until no new themes or concepts emerged. Codes created towards the end of the second cycle were applied to transcripts that were coded earlier during the second cycle; likewise, transcripts that were coded late in the second cycle were reviewed for consistency with codes that were created early within the second cycle. Several new codes were also generated at this stage and were applied across all transcripts when applicable. Through working iteratively in this way, I ensured the consistent application of codes across the data and reached data saturation.

The Lexical Search tool (available in the **Analysis** menu) was used at this stage to create a code for every instance of a particular word that I had identified as central to my research. Early on in my fieldwork, my interlocutors surprised me by arguing that "indiscipline" and

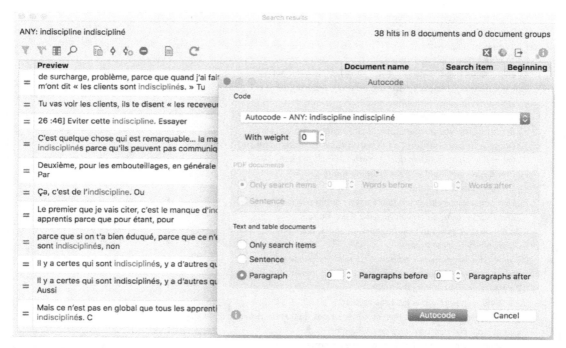

Fig. 5:   The Lexical Search tool identified 38 unique instances of the French terms "indiscipline" and "indiscipliné" in the data, which were then auto-coded with a weight of 0

"undisciplined" people were the root cause of Dakar's public transportation woes. Recognizing the concept as interesting and important, I began probing deeply on the meaning of these terms with my respondents whenever it came up in conversation. Although I could have coded for "indiscipline" and its adjective forms manually, I chose to perform a Lexical Search so that no instances of it were accidentally missed or omitted. The Lexical Search returned 38 instances of the word in my data set (Fig. 5), which resulted in 24 auto-coded segments named "indiscipline."

When choosing the amount of text to be auto-coded in Lexical Search, I opted to code the entire paragraph in which the terms "indiscipline" or "indiscipliné(e)(s)" occurred (Fig. 5). Because I was primarily concerned with understanding exactly what it meant to be "undisciplined" in and outside of the context of public transportation, coding the full paragraph in which the term occurred set the groundwork for future analysis using visual tools, and in particular the Code Relations Browser.

5   Organization of the code system

Organization of my code system was left until the end of the third coding cycle. Because I had coded openly, my code system was one long, unorganized list of hundreds of codes. This is a common result when working with grounded theory or initial coding, as codes are created quickly and tentatively for further refinement or organization at later stages in the analytical process.

The code system was first sorted alphabetically to quickly identify duplicate codes which were then merged. Codes with one or two coded segments within them were reviewed for their relevance to the central research question and kept or deleted on a case-by-case basis.

Next, the Overview of Coded Segments and Smart Coding Tool were utilized to further distill nebulous categories such as "indiscipline." Although I had probed my informants specifically on what, exactly, it meant to be "*indiscipliné,*" I still wanted to understand the personal qualities and behaviors that were associated with "undisciplined" behavior, and, further, how these behaviors and qualities impacted my informants' view of the modernization of public transportation.

After auto-coding for "indiscipline" via the Lexical Search, I opened the Overview of Coded Segments by right-clicking the code in my code system. From there, I selected the **Smart Coding Tool** icon in the top toolbar. The Smart Coding Tool is a dynamic work environment in which one can review the coded segments in any given category. Concurrent codes may also be viewed here, and codes can be added to or deleted from the segments.

In the Smart Coding Tool, I reviewed each "indiscipline" segment for relevance and reviewed the other thematic and descriptive codes that co-occurred with each segment (Fig. 6). I created new codes when I identified a theme that had not been initially coded and applied it to the segments in which that theme appeared. In other instances, pre-existing codes were applied to the segments in instances where the code may have been mistakenly missed in the second coding cycle. This process enabled me to further investigate the notion of "indiscipline" and other abstract codes by categorizing them into smaller sub-themes and categories.

Document	Coded Segments	Codes
Adama, Pos. 16	Mais surtout la surcharge, il faut qu'ils arrêtent de surcharger les bus parce qu'on a connu quand même un évènement très très scandaleux, le bateau le joola, [8 :15] aujourd'hui on avait dit même avec Wade il ne fallait plus surcharger que ce soit en tout cas les véhicules dans tous les secteurs que ce soit terrestre, que ce soit maritime, que ce soit [unheard] donc tout ça il faut régler ce problème. Problème de surcharge, problème, parce que quand j'ai fait ce reportage les receveurs m'ont dit « les clients sont indisciplinés. » Tu vas voir les clients, ils te disent « les receveurs sont indisciplinés. » Donc il y a toujours un problème de communication, problème de compréhension souvent qui se posent. Avec les chauffeurs dans les Tatas, on n'a pas de problème.	Education Abdoulaye Wade ...Experience\Receveurs ...Experience\Clients/Passengers ...Experience\Overcrowding ...Experience\le Joola Lack of Communication ...of Transit\TATA
Adama, Pos. 38	La correction, la discipline, qu'ils soient encrés par toute la population.	Education Bidonvilles/Suburbs Change Public Mentality Development Poverty
Adama, Pos. 40	Mais c'est pas suffisant. Il faut faire tout le monde, il faut faire des choses en tout cas, il va nous conduire au développement, essayer de changer des—moi, je suis toujours pour le changement de mentalité. Donc, j'ai eu à faire partie du club modèle, le club modèle [unheard] c'est pour les actions citoyennes. Donc c'était ça. Aller sur les plages, durant l'été. Donc c'était ce genre d'activité il faut qu'on voit ça un peu partout. Sensibiliser les gens. Leur disent également si vous buvez une tasse de café il faut pas jeter ça dans la rue. [26 :46] Eviter cette indiscipline. Essayer d'avoir beaucoup de corrections. On s'améliore quand même dans les habitudes et tout ça mais il faut encore de la formation, recycler les populations. Dans les secteurs, il faut les renforcements des capacités dans les entreprises parce que souvent on peut recruter quelqu'un avec Bac +2, Bac +4, mais est-ce que réellement il a les attitudes pour faire vraiment bien le travail ?	Education Change Public Mentality Development Public behavior Sensibiliser/Sensibilisation

Fig. 6:   The Smart Coding Tool was used to review coded segments in any given code, review other codes that are applied to the segment concurrently, and to add, delete, or refine codes as needed

The code system was then further organized and refined into top-level categories with sub-categories using the **Codes > Creative Coding** tool. Although codes can be organized into hierarchies directly in the Code System window itself, I prefer the Creative Coding tool because its interactive nature allows one to drag and drop codes around the screen, think through relationships, and save the results as a map in MAXMaps, which may be used later in the analytical process to further visualize relationships between themes and concepts.

Many of the codes created during my second and third cycles were also descriptive in nature and catalogued aspects of the public transportation experience, from waiting for the bus, to the bus' routes and timetables, and cost of fare. These codes were brought into the Creative Coding tool and grouped thematically under the top-level category "Bus Journey/Experience" (Fig. 7). For example, the codes "theft," "fights/disputes," "old/dilapidated vehicles," and "traffic accidents" were grouped together and added as sub-codes under the new category "safety." "Safety" was then linked to "Bus Journey/Experience" as a second level sub-category.

Through grouping my descriptive codes thematically and by linking them as second, third, or even fourth level codes underneath "Bus Journey/Experience," I created a network of codes that described the various dimensions of traveling on and operating public transportation. These codes and their respective segments later became the backbone of my ethnographic account of the *car rapide* in Dakar.

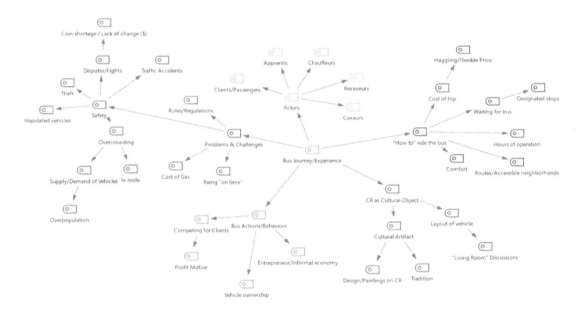

Fig. 7: Descriptive codes capturing the various dimensions of public transportation (safety, actors involved, behavior, culture, etc.) were arranged thematically in the Creative Coding tool. Directional arrows imply hierarchy, and the established hierarchy is saved and applied to the Code System in the form of codes and sub-codes

6 Memos

Throughout my coding and analytical processes, I relied extensively on writing document memos. Memos have a broad application in MAXQDA and can be applied at multiple levels of the project, including directly to documents or codes. I predominantly utilize in-document memos as a way to capture and categorize my thoughts, questions, and theories as I work through the data. Although the majority of my memos were "free" memos without any label, I also utilized ? memos to document questions I had about particular references made by my respondents. The ! memo type was used sparingly to mark particularly important information with follow-up thoughts. Because my data was collected in my non-native language, I also occasionally used memos to define Senegalese French colloquialisms and other language that I was not immediately familiar with.

Although many of my memos were short in length, they served as powerful "notes to self" and, on more than one occasion, helped inform or jumpstart sections of my final thesis. Take, for example, the memo in Fig. 8; just 2 sentences in length, this memo ultimately represented one of the most important opinions expressed by my interlocutors and, consequently, one of the most important themes underlying their view of the modernization of public transportation in Dakar.

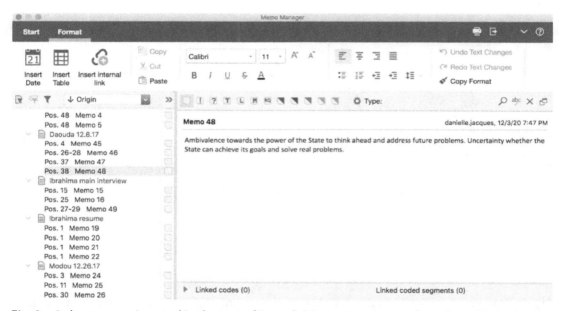

Fig. 8:   A short memo inserted in the text of Daouda's interview captured my thoughts in the moment, and later became an important analytical tool as I thought through my data set and began writing the final thesis

7   Analysis

I began my analysis of coded data with the Code Relations Browser from the **Visual Tools** menu. The Code Relations Browser is a visual representation of the frequency of overlapping codes and aids in the identification of patterns and relationships in the data.

Because I had structured my coding so that thematic codes were superimposed on top of descriptive highlight codes, the Code Relations Browser enabled me to compare and contrast the "journey/experience" on each type of bus. This was achieved by first activating the descriptive highlight codes in the Code System window, and then by setting the Code Relations Browser rows to "all codes" and the columns to "all activated codes."

The resulting output allowed me to view the frequency at which codes such as "safety" were mentioned in relation to the 4 main types of public transit. This visual representation of themes was critical in the composition of my ethnography of the *car rapide*; at a glance, I was able to compare and contrast the buses and identify the most common "problems" on each bus, as reported by my respondents. For example, Fig. 9 clearly shows that "safety" and "overcrowding" were a larger concern for respondents on the *car rapide* than it was for them on the *Dem Dikk* or the *Tata* buses.

Fig. 9:   The Code Relations Browser enables the researcher to visualize the frequency of overlaps between two codes. Here, descriptive highlight codes (columns) are analyzed with thematic codes (rows) to quickly visualize the frequency of codes such as "safety" across several modes of public transportation

While the Code Relations Browser was key in identifying patterns and in comparing and contrasting my interlocutors' experiences on each type of bus, the results in the Browser lack the color and detail that would come to inform my ethnographic account of public transportation in Dakar. In other words, while the output told me that "disputes/fights" were discussed more frequently when referring to the *car rapide* than to the *Dem Dikk* or the *Tata*, it did not provide any context behind this relationship. Therefore, to answer questions such as "What *types* of fights and disputes does one encounter on the *car rapide*? How do these fights differ from those you find on the *Dem Dikk* and *Tata*?" I had to conduct further analysis using the Complex Coding Query tool.

The Complex Coding Query tool is accessed via MAXQDA's **Analysis** tab in the tool ribbon. The tool retrieves coded segments of text using a variety of nuanced functions. Whereas the Retrieved Segments window will, by default, simply list coded segments of text in one or more activated categories, the Complex Coding Query allows one to perform a complex search for coded segments based on two or more specified criteria. Therefore, in order to identify the segments of text in my dataset that were coded <u>both</u> as "*car rapide*" <u>and</u> as "disputes/fights," it was not enough to activate both codes in my Code System window—doing so would result in a long list of segments coded as "*car rapide*," followed by a list of all segments coded as "disputes/fights." Instead, I conducted an "overlapping" Complex Coding Query using both codes "*car rapide*" and "disputes/fights" (Fig. 10). This function resulted in 19 segments that contained both codes. The results were then reviewed directly in the Retrieved Segments window, and I took physical written notes on the findings.

The process of identifying patterns in the Code Relations Browser, adding color and context to these patterns using the Complex Coding Query, and reviewing the results in the Retrieved Segments window was repeated countless times for each new relationship identified throughout the analysis phase of my research. Although coding had officially ended by this phase in the research, I added segments to the "Great Quotes" category as I worked through the data and identified important quotes to be used in the final thesis.

8   Lessons learned

My research journey was a highly iterative process in which I constantly created, applied, and refined codes and categories. These categories were later explored on a case-by-case basis first using the Code Relations Browser to identify patterns, and subsequently using Complex Coding Queries to add context and detail to these patterns. To that end, the Retrieved Segments window was the most important and most utilized analytical tool in my project.

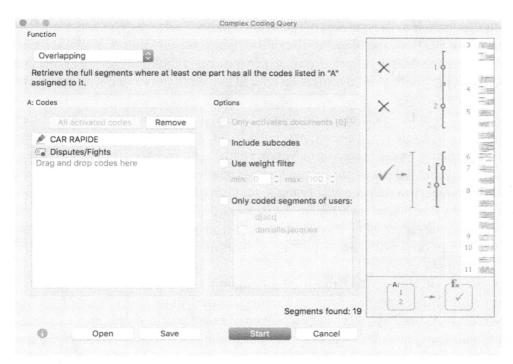

Fig. 10: The Complex Coding Query tool is used to identify segments of text which have all of the codes listed in section A; in this case, the tool has identified 19 segments that were coded with *both* "CAR RAPIDE" and "disputes/fights"

Admittedly, my analytical process was influenced by my chosen coding strategies, and especially by the quality of my codes themselves. Although I refined and categorized my codes in several cycles and using various tools, there may have been opportunities to refine my codes even further; for example, with "disputes/fights," a Complex Coding Query or Overview of Coded Segments could have been avoided had I better refined the category upfront during my coding cycles. In other words, rather than reviewing coded segments to distill the various types of disputes one might find on a *car rapide*, I could have preemptively coded each type rather than lumping them all into one large "bucket."

Saldaña (2016) notes that initial coding, my chosen second-cycle coding strategy, may "alert the researcher that more data are needed to support and build an emerging theory" (p. 115). Indeed, I found this to be the case as I worked through my dataset and became increasingly interested in my interlocutors' notion of "indiscipline." The frequency of a given code may not necessarily correspond with its importance or relevance to the research question; "indiscipline" accounted for just 24 coded segments out of a total 1,200 (accounting for just 2% of all coded segments). Nevertheless, these 24 segments ultimately proved fruitful in describing how Dakarois envision "indiscipline" on public transportation in the city. However, they fell short of fully describing how "indiscipline" in the public sphere is linked to their understanding of "good governance," state responsibility, and development in the post-colonial context. Given the tight time constraints of my MA program, returning to the field to collect more data proved impossible, but this gap in the data leaves the door open for further investigation should I go on to pursue a doctorate degree in the future.

Furthermore, because many of the tools in MAXQDA can be accessed 2 or sometimes even 3 different ways, one may access a particular function or tool one way, only to later discover an alternative way of accessing or working with that tool. For example, my process of first using the Code Relations Browser to identify relationships and then conducting a Complex Coding Query to pull corresponding segments could have been simplified, had I known at the time that double-clicking on the square or circle icon in the Code Relations Browser will automatically pull up those intersecting segments in the Retrieved Segments window, without the need of actually pulling up the Complex Coding Query dialog and manually running the query.[1]

The biggest lesson learned from this mini-ethnography, however, is that MAXQDA is a truly dynamic tool that can flex to meet the needs and unique work style of the researcher—there is no one "right" or "wrong" way to leverage its analytical and visual tools. Even today, with four years of MAXQDA experience under my belt, I am still learning new ways of accessing and utilizing the various tools in the software. While I perhaps could have been more thorough in refining certain codes upfront in my coding process, or saved time by double-clicking in the Code Relations Browser rather than running a separate Complex Coding Query, my processes still enabled me to arrive at a robust analysis of the data, a thesis I am proud of, and a strong foundational knowledge of MAXQDA's functions that I continue to build upon and draw from today as I use the software in a professional capacity as a MAXQDA trainer and market researcher.

Bibliography

Birks, M., & Mills, J. (2015). *Grounded theory: A practical guide.* Sage.

Kuckartz, U. (2014). *Qualitative text analysis: A guide to methods, practice & using software.* Sage.

Kuckartz, U., & Rädiker, S. (2019). *Analyzing qualitative data with MAXQDA: Text, audio, and video.* Springer Nature Switzerland. https://doi.org/10.1007/978-3-030-15671-8

Saldaña, J. (2016). *The coding manual for qualitative researchers* (3rd ed.). Sage.

---

1   It should be noted, however, that double-clicking in the Code Relations Browser will result in an "intersection" complex query. The Complex Coding Query will therefore need to be used when the researcher wishes to conduct a query based on other attributes (such as "overlapping," "near," etc.), or when the researcher is also interested in filtering by weight or by user.

About the author

Danielle N. Jacques is a professional MAXQDA trainer and consultant. She holds an MA in Social Science from the University of Chicago and a BA in Sociology and French & Franco-phone Studies from Clark University. She has been a user of MAXQDA since 2017 and has used it for a variety of projects, from international development to market research.

Using MAXQDA in Qualitative Content Analysis: An Example Comparing Single-Person and Focus Group Interviews

Natalie Santos, Vera Monteiro, Lourdes Mata

Abstract

This chapter illustrates a qualitative project aimed at understanding the similarities and disparities that occur when students' and teachers' conceptions of assessment are compared. We used a multiple-case study design, with five third grade teachers and their students. The data were gathered through both single-person (with teachers) and focus group (with students) interviews. The purpose of this chapter is to provide a detailed description of how the visual tools of MAXQDA were used to compare how elementary Portuguese teachers and students conceive mathematics assessment. We present this case illustration in four sections. The first section contains the background, objectives, and guiding methodology of the project. The second section describes the preparation of the data and the development of the coding system by using both concept-driven and data-driven categories. In the third section, we explain how we compared and contrasted all summarized data in terms of categories by using the MAXQDA visual tools: Document Portrait, Code Matrix Browser, and Code Relations Browser. The final section describes how we used the Summary Grid and the Summary Tables to organize our findings and draw our conclusions. We conclude with a review of the pros and cons of alternative ways of comparing single-person and focus group interviews using MAXQDA.

Key MAXQDA features covered

✓ Coding   ✓ Code Matrix Browser

✓ MAXMaps   ✓ Code Relations Browser

✓ Document Portrait   ✓ Summary Grid and Tables

1 Introduction

There are different approaches to classroom assessment. The predominant one in schools is Assessment OF Learning (AoL). Its purpose is to certify learning and report students' progress in school to parents and students, thereby promoting extrinsic motivation and social comparison. Assessment FOR Learning (AfL) is designed to assist teachers and students in improving teaching and learning by providing them with specific feedback that both need to make adjustments to the learning process (Azis, 2015). Students and teachers believe that assessment is crucial for the efficiency of teaching and learning processes and a shared understanding of the purposes of assessment in meeting learning and teaching goals. This shared understanding of what is being worked on is essential to help students learn from their learning experiences (Andersson, 2016). In teacher-and-student interactions and peer interactions, knowledge acquisition is dependent on the shared representation of the task and the context of learning. According to Gipps (1999) and Andersson (2016), assessment can be viewed as an intersubjectivity setting, where shared understanding between teacher and student is central to learning outcomes. Carless (2009) states that such shared understanding improves assessment integrity and the quality of student learning experiences. Therefore, it is essential that student and teacher conceptions of assessment are aligned.

Few studies have compared teachers' and their students' assessment conceptions (e.g., Brown, 2008; Remesal, 2006). These previous researchers have found that, in general, their conceptions differ. While students have a clear conception that assessment has a fundamental purpose—the certification of student learning—teachers' conceptions of assessment are somewhat unclear but show a strong tendency toward the purpose of improving teaching and learning (Remesal, 2006). Since teachers and students are directly involved in the same pedagogical process, including assessment, it is strange that they perceive it as having different purposes.

Our study is part of a larger research project that aimed to study how teachers' and students' conceptions of assessment and teachers' assessment practices were related to students' outcomes. In particular, we sought to explore the conceptions that Portuguese elementary teachers and students have of assessment and investigate whether these conceptions are aligned. We used MAXQDA's tools to help us in our research process.

2   Data collection and methodological approach

Since our goal was to describe the common meaning for teachers' and students' experiences about assessment, we used a phenomenological approach. This methodology allows the researcher to explore how a phenomenon, experience, or concept—in this case, assessment in mathematics—is described by the participants (Creswell & Poth, 2018). Therefore, it focused on descriptions, perceptions, and explanations of a phenomenon.

We used a descriptive multiple-case design (Chmiliar, 2012) to develop a more indepth understanding of teachers' and students' conceptions of assessment. The cases were five third-grade classes (A, B, C, D, and E) from four Portuguese primary schools, selected purposely in advance. We looked for a maximum variation sampling in teachers' experience and gender to elicit a wider range of responses (Guest, Namey, & Mitchell,

2013). Therefore, teachers who participated (one male and four females) had between 3 and 25 years of experience and class size ranged from 11 to 23 students (82 third-grade class students in total).

The data were gathered both single-person interviews with teachers, and focus group sessions with students. The conversations with teachers, with an approximate duration of 45 minutes each, addressed 5 assessment topics based on the literature (Azis, 2015; Remesal, 2006): (1) definition, (2) targets, (3) purposes, (4) practices, and (5) criteria. The individual interviews were experience focused (Brinkmann, 2013) to elicit accurate reports of teachers' experiences regarding assessment. The conversations with students, with an approximate duration of 30 minutes, were conducted with groups of four to five students (two groups for Class D, three groups each for Classes B and E, and four groups each for Classes A and C). Only three assessment topics were addressed in the focus groups to maintain children's concentration: (1) definition, (2) purposes, and (3) practices. Our objective was not to reach consensus but to collect all students' experiences and beliefs about assessment. Therefore, the focus group moderator kept the discussion informative rather than argumentative, ensuring the participation of all students.

3 Data Analysis with MAXQDA

3.1 Preparation of the data

All single-person interviews and focus group discussions were audio-recorded and transcribed verbatim in Microsoft Word documents. Each single-person transcript was imported to the MAXQDA project as a single document. All focus group transcriptions of the same class were imported together into one individual document. For example, in the single document "Students A" we had the transcription of the four focus group discussions performed with the students of class A. We organized the data in this way so that we had two documents for class, representing the two sets of individuals that we aimed to compare—students and teachers. Consequently, our project had in the Document System ten documents, five with teachers' data, and five with students' data, organized into five document groups, one for each class (Fig. 1).

Document memos were used to describe information about the context of the interview and other methodological aspects that could be relevant to the research or could have an impact on the research process. Keeping records of this information was very important for reporting the findings and assessing the quality and reliability of data collection.

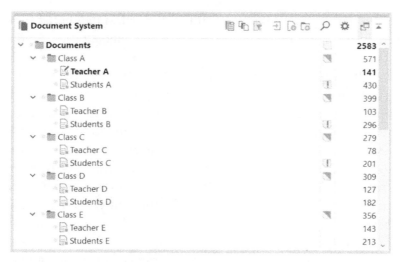

Fig. 1: Document System

3.2 The coding process

Step one in our coding process was to create what Saldaña (2013) calls utilitarian or structural codes. This type of coding allowed us to label and index the content of the documents so that we could quickly access and limit the extraction to the data relevant to a particular analysis. Two groups of structural codes were created. One group represented the topics of the interviews that is being discussed (*Definition, Targets, Purposes, Practices*, and *Criteria*). Since we had several focus group transcriptions in the same document, we created a second group identifying the focus groups in each students' document (*Focus Groups 1, 2, 3,* and *4*) so we could differentiate the contribution of each group. These structural codes were created in the MAXQDA's Code System as sub-codes of the top-level codes *Topics* and *Focus Group* (see the complete code system in Fig. 2). The code memos of the *Topics* codes were used to register the interview questions of each topic. We coded the corresponding text passages of each document using these structural codes.

No labeling was used to identify individual student's names in the focus group discussion because our analyses did not focus on students' individual conceptions but on their views as a group. Yet, MAXQDA provides options for importing focus group transcriptions that automatically code the contributions made to the discussion by each participant. This coding provides easy access to the development of the stated opinions of individuals when the researcher is interested in analyzing focus groups at the individual level.

Once we coded our documents with the structural codes, we performed a content analysis of the data. We used data-driven descriptive codes to code what the participant(s) said in a manifest analysis, staying very close to the text and describing its visible and apparent content (Bengtsson, 2016). These led to a plethora of codes that were combined into smaller groups of closely related codes to create sub-categories. Later, these sub-categories were organized in both concept-driven and data-driven categories with a latent analysis in which we tried to find the underlying meaning of the participants' discourse (Bengtsson, 2016).

Starting with the typology of assessment conceptions previously described by Brown (2008, 2013, 2018) (Assessment for (1) improvement, (2) school's accountability, and (3) students' accountability), categories and sub-categories were progressively redefined through a cyclical process, creating new categories when necessary to fit the reality of our data (Miles, Huberman, & Saldaña, 2014).

Fig. 2: Final code system

Fig. 3 presents a concept map created in MAXMaps (**Visual Tools > MAXMaps**) with the conceptions described by Brown (2008, 2013, 2018) and our final four categories. The categories *Students' Accountability* and *Improvement of Learning and Teaching* were very similar to those described by Brown (2008, 2013, 2018). Our *External Reporting* category had some similarities to Brown's *School's Accountability* conception since our participants considered that assessment involved some type of external reporting. Still, the school and teachers' accountability was not as present in our participants' discourse as in Brown's assessment conceptions, so we highlight this difference in the name of the category. *Externally Motivating Students* was a data-driven category, defined inductively from the data. The sub-categories are also represented in Fig. Fig. 3. The widths of the linking lines indicate the frequency at which these sub-categories were assigned in the participants' discourse.

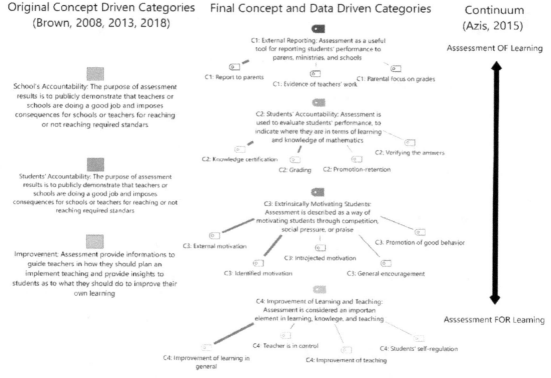

Fig. 3: Visualization of the Assessment Conceptions' categories using the MAXMaps Hierarchical Code-Subcodes Model

The categories and sub-categories were organized in the MAXQDA's Code System as subcodes of the top-level code *Assessment Conceptions* (see Fig. 2). The order of the categories was based on the literature (Azis, 2015). We organized our categories within a continuum that moves between an assessment OF learning pole (AoL, with a greater focus on certification and accountability) and an assessment FOR learning pole (AfL, with greater emphasis on improving learning and teaching) (see Fig. 3). We assigned different colors for each category. The colors helped us to differentiate between different conceptions in the visual analysis tools. Code memos were used to describe the meaning of a category as clearly as possible (including their theoretical background, inclusion and exclusion criteria of application, examples, and differentiation from other categories).

Our unit of analysis was a unit of meaning (i.e., one or more consecutive sentences with a common meaning). Consequently, the categories and sub-categories were applied to pieces of text with the same meaning that could include several sentences or several participants' interactions in the focus group interviews. For example, in Fig. 4, we observed several comments from three Class A students, who defined assessment as the practice of assigning grades and marks to students' work. Therefore, all the interactions between the three students were coded with the sub-category *Grading* and its respective category, *Students' Accountability*. In Fig. 4, we can see that there are 4 coding stripes: one for the topic been discussed (Assessment definition, in black), one to identify the group that we are analyzing (Focus group 1, also in black), one for the assessment conception category and one for the sub-category (both in blue). Any block of data could be coded simultaneously only with sub-categories of the same category of assessment conceptions. We only coded units of meaning that were relevant to our research questions. Henceforth, not every portion of the interviews' transcripts was coded. The categories and sub-categories were carefully cross-examined by three external researchers and found to be descriptive of the data. For intercoder consistency, a second coder, working as a supervisor, confirmed the analyses of the first coder. Discrepancies were discussed by three external researchers.

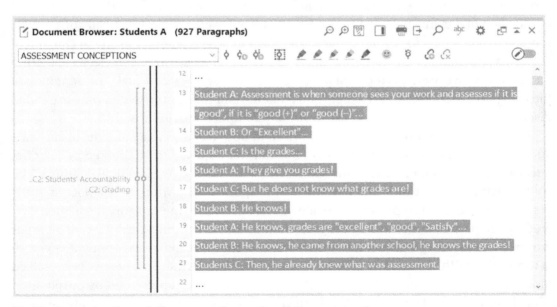

Fig. 4:   Example of a coded segment from a Focus Group Interview

3.3 Visualizing our results

In this section, we explain how we compared and contrasted all summarized data in terms of categories by using the MAXQDA visual tools Document Portrait, Code Matrix Browser, and Code Relations Browser. For the sake of simplicity, we only illustrate how these specific tools were used in two of the cases analyzed: one where teacher's and students' conceptions were aligned (Class A) and one where they were not (Class C).

The Document Portrait: How extensively was a category discussed?

We applied MAXQDA's Document Portrait to visualize the category that was the most often talked about by the participant(s) during the interview, that is, to assess the relative time over which the categories were discussed or mentioned. This visual tool represents code segments with a certain number of tiles with the color of the corresponding code. The number of tiles depends on the length of the coded segments, so the image can indicate the relative amount of time the categories were discussed or mentioned. This visual tool is only useful if we have assigned colors to the codes following a logical scheme. In our case, we used very distinct colors for each category (and respective sub-categories) of assessment conception, so we can quickly notice how much the participants talk about a specific topic.

The Document Portrait (**Visual Tools > Document Portrait**) displays the document currently open in the Document Browser (a single-person interview or a collection of focus group discussions) as an image of the activated coded segments, ordered according to the researcher's preference. Because our categories and sub-categories overlap and to avoid duplication of the area for a code in the image, we only activated the four categories of the top-level code *Assessment Conceptions*. MAXQDA allows us to open as many Document Portrait as documents are in the Document System and place them alongside each other on the screen. We used this tool first because it creates a very clear visual representation of the categories mentioned by teachers and students and the approximated time expended discussing each one, so it is very easy to visually compare both groups.

In Fig. 5, we present the Document Portrait of both teachers and students of classes A and C. The appearance of the Document Portrait was adjusted to be **Ordered by color frequency**, meaning that the tiles of the same color were stacked as individual columns. The column with the most tiles (the one with the largest coded portion of the document) is placed on the left. This representation allowed us to visualize the category most often covered by the participant(s) during the interview. Since we kept the transcripts of all focus groups per class in a single document, we can also compare the coded segment coverage of the teacher with his/her students. We can see, for example, that Teacher of Class A talked more about the *External Reporting* functions of assessment, represented by purple tiles, while his/her students mentioned this category very little. Teacher of Class A also spoke a lot about assessment as a tool for *Students' Accountability*—the category most mentioned by his/her students. For Class C, the teacher's discourse was most often focused on *Improvement,* while students focused on *Students' Accountability*. If we wanted to know the exact percentage of coded segments in each category, we could complement the information provided by the Document Portrait with the Code Coverage function (**Analysis > Code Coverage > Texts, Tables and PDFs**). This feature indicates the number of characters coded in the document with our assessment conceptions categories and can calculate percentages based on the total characters in the document (**Percentages of the entire text**) or based only on the coded characters (**Percentages of "coded"**).

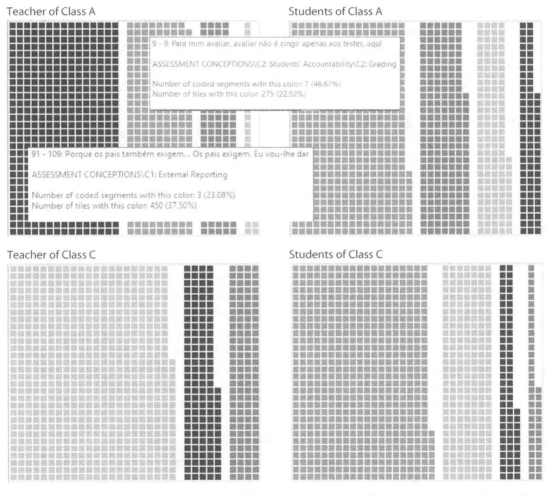

Fig. 5: Visualization of the category most often using MAXQDA's Document Portrait (Sorting by color frequency, with 900 tiles). Purple = External Reporting; blue = Students' Accountability; red = Externally Motivating Students; green = Improvement of Learning and Teaching

One useful aspect of the Document Portrait feature is that it creates not only a representation of the time the categories were discussed but also indicates how many times a unit of analysis was coded with the same color. This information indicates the number of times a category was reintroduced into the discussion during the interview. This data is displayed when you hover your cursor over a tile with the color of interest (see boxes displayed in Fig. 5). These are the same values displayed by the Code Matrix Browser (see next section). For example, in Fig. 5, for Teacher of Class A the number of coded segments with purple (*External Reporting*) was three (23% of the coded segments in the document evaluated for the Document Portrait). Conversely, the topic *Students' Accountability* (in blue) was mentioned seven times (54% of the evaluated coded segments). It seems that Teacher A spent more time talking about *External Reporting* (there were more characters coded with this category), but she/he keeps bringing back to the discussion the *Students' Accountability* category during the interview. Hence, the information reported in the boxes provided valuable information for our analysis, especially considering how we coded the focus group data. Since one segment code could include several sentences and several students' interactions as long as they remained on the same category, extensive coverage could be observed even when the participants were just repeating or rephrasing each other's ideas, with little contribution to the discussion. In addition, since the names of the speakers were coded ("Student A," "Student B," and "Student C", as shown in Fig. 4), it was possible that we artificially increased the length of their contributions. Therefore, we needed to continue exploring our data.

The Code Matrix Browser: How often was a category or sub-category mentioned?

We employed the Code Matrix Browser (**Visual Tools > Code Matrix Browser**) to visualize the categories and all the specific aspects of the categories (or sub-categories) that the participants discussed. This tool creates a matrix with activated documents in the columns and activated codes in the rows. The Code Matrix Browser displays how many times the codes were assigned to a document (see Fig. 6). A square indicates if the code was present in the document or not, and the size of the square indicates how many times it was mentioned. In Fig. 6, the symbol sizes were calculated considering the total frequency of coded segments in the document (i.e., by column), so the frequency was relativized. If we click on the symbol **Display nodes as values**, we can view information about how many times the codes were assigned to a document. This is the same information that was accessible in the Document Portrait when one's cursor hovers over a tile.

We thought that if (nearly) all sub-categories of an assessment conception category were present in a document, it would indicate the richness of the content addressed by the participants, reflecting how deeply they had thought about specific aspects of assessment. For example, the teacher's discourse from Class A about *External Reporting* was very rich, mentioning several aspects about how she/he used assessment for external reporting.

Conversely, the discourse on *Students' Accountability* was limited to the aspects of students' *Grading*. The Code Matrix Browser also allowed us to easily compare the teacher's interviews with their students' focus group discussions. In contrast to their teacher, students of Class A had a more detailed description of the assessment aspects related to *Students' Accountability*. They also mentioned almost all sub-categories of the *Externally Motivating Students* and the *Improvement of Learning and Teaching* categories. In addition, this display allowed us to recognize that even if both the teacher of Class C and his/her students mentioned most of the sub-categories of the *Improvement* category, the teacher mentioned such more times than the students (the symbol of the nodes in the Teacher of Class C document are larger than the nodes of his/her students).

Code System	Teacher A	Students A	Teacher C	Students C	SUM
ASSESSMENT CONCEPTIONS					0
C1: External Reporting	■	■	·	■	18
C1: Report to parents	■	■	·	·	16
C1: Parental focus on grades	■		·		3
C1: Evidence of teachers' work	·			·	2
C2: Students' Accountability	■	■		■	67
C2: Knowledge certification		■		■	19
C2: Grading	■	■		■	34
C2: Promotion-retention		■		■	35
C2: Verifying the answers		■		■	18
C3: Extrinsically Motivating Students	·	■	■	■	31
C3: Identified motivation		■	■	■	15
C3: Promotion of good behavior		■			7
C3: External motivation	·	·		■	7
C3: Introjected motivation	·				4
C3: General encouragement					0
C4: Improvement of Learning and Teaching	■	■	■	■	26
C4: Teacher is in control		■	■	·	12
C4: Improvement of teaching	·		■	■	7
C4: Students' self-regulation		·	■		9
C4: Improvement of learning in general	·	·		·	5
SUM	28	199	23	85	335

Fig. 6: Visualization of the category most mentioned by the participants using MAXQDA's Code Matrix Browser (relativized by column)

Having all the focus groups in one document allowed us to compare teachers' and students' conceptions easily. However, we do not know if all four focus group discussions we performed with students of Class A were consistent in their views about assessment (because in the same document were between two to four different focus groups transcriptions). Fortunately, by clicking on the **Interactive Quote Matrix** icon 🖾 (first one on the left), we had access to all the coded segments in the categories. These coded segments include information about the source, highlighted in blue. By selecting such, we had access to the corresponding section within the document displayed in the Document Browser, and we could see the segment in its original context. Therefore, we could check which focus group mentioned the category or sub-category. Still, this was an arduous task, so we decided to use the Code Relations Browser to assess the consistency of our results with a more rapid and straightforward approach.

The Code Relations Browser: When and by whom were the categories mentioned?

Each document in our Document Browser was coded with three sets of codes: One group of structural codes identified the interview *Topic* that was being discussed by the participants; another identified which group of students' interactions we were analyzing in the students' documents (remember that there were between two to four different focus groups in the same document); and the last related to the categories and sub-categories of *Assessment Conceptions*. Therefore, in students' documents, three codes could be assigned to the same text, identifying what they said about assessment, which group of students said it, and when. Therefore, if we wanted to know which focus group mentioned the assessment categories, we needed to analyze the co-occurrence of codes in students' documents. This was done with the Code Relations Browser that generates matrices code by code of one or several documents.

In Fig. 7, we display part of the Code Relations Browser for the students of Class A document (**Visual Tools > Code Relations Browser**). We activated the *Assessment Conceptions* codes and the *Focus Group* codes, and we chose the **Intersections** option in the context menu. As we can see, all focus groups mentioned the sub-categories of *Students' Accountability* and *Externally Motivating Students'* categories. Only Focus Group 3 mentioned several sub-categories of the *Improvement* category. Therefore, the conception of assessment as a useful tool for *Improvement* was not consistently present in all focus group discussions.

Besides assessing the consistency of results through the different focus groups, the Code Relations Browser also allowed us to visualize the category with the most consistent presence in the single-person/focus group discussion (i.e., the one mentioned throughout nearly all topics of conversation). We created one display for each document, activating the *Assessment Conceptions* categories and *Topics* of interview codes, choosing the **Intersection of codes in a segment** option. In Fig. 8, we observe that even the Document Portrait and the Code Matrix Browser indicated that the discourse of Teacher of Class A was more extensive and richer regarding the *External Reporting* purpose of assessment, the Code Relations Browser indicated that this category was only mentioned at the end of the interview. The category that was systematically mentioned through all interviews was *Students'*

Accountability. Similarly, for students, the most mentioned category in all topics was *Students' Accountability,* although the *Externally Motivating Students* was also present in all topics, but not as often.

Code System	Focus Group 1	Focus Group 2	Focus Group 3	Focus Group 4	SUM
> FOCUS GROUP #					0
∨ ASSESSMENT CONCEPTIONS					0
∨ C1: External Reporting		·	■	■	11
C1: Report to parents		·	■	■	11
C1: Parental focus on grades					0
C1: Evidence of teachers' work					0
∨ C2: Students' Accountability	■	■	■	■	42
C2: Knowledge certification		·	■	·	12
C2: Grading	■	■	■	■	20
C2: Promotion-retention	■	■	■	■	23
C2: Verifying the answers	■	·	■	■	13
∨ C3: Extrinsically Motivating Students	■		■	■	21
C3: Identified motivation	■		■	·	9
C3: Promotion of good behavior			■	■	7
C3: External motivation			·	·	3
C3: Introjected motivation			■	·	4
C3: General encouragement					0
∨ C4: Improvement of Learning and Teaching	·	·	■	·	11
C4: Teacher is in control		·	·	·	8
C4: Improvement of teaching					0
C4: Students' self-regulation			·		2
C4: Improvement of learning in general			·		2
SUM	34	19	94	52	199

Fig. 7: Visualization of the categories and sub-categories mentioned in each focus group discussion of Class A, using MAXQDA's Code Relations Browser

Teacher

Code System	Assessment Practices	Assessment Definition	Assessment Targets	Assessment Purposes	Assessment Criteria
> TOPICS					
∨ ASSESSMENT CONCEPTIONS					
C1: External Reporting				■	■
C2: Students' Accountability	■	■		■	■
C3: Extrinsically Motivating Students				■	
C4: Improvement of Learning and Teaching	■		■		
SUM	2	1	1	3	6

Students A

Code System	Assessment Practices	Assessment Definition	Assessment Targets	Assessment Purposes	Assessment Criteria
> TOPICS					
∨ ASSESSMENT CONCEPTIONS					
C1: External Reporting				■	
C2: Students' Accountability	■	■		■	
C3: Extrinsically Motivating Students	·	■		■	
C4: Improvement of Learning and Teaching			■	■	
SUM	8	23	0	54	0

Fig. 8: Visualization of the category with the most consistent presence in the interview of Teacher A and his/her students using MAXQDA's Code Relations Browser

Further, since we had more than one focus group per class, we needed to assess the consistency of the results by observing each focus group separately. Using the Code Relations Browser option **Only for segments of the following code**, we limited the search to segments of one focus group at a time, as shown in Fig. 9. The matrix confirmed that the category consistently mentioned by all groups in all topics was *Students' Accountability*.

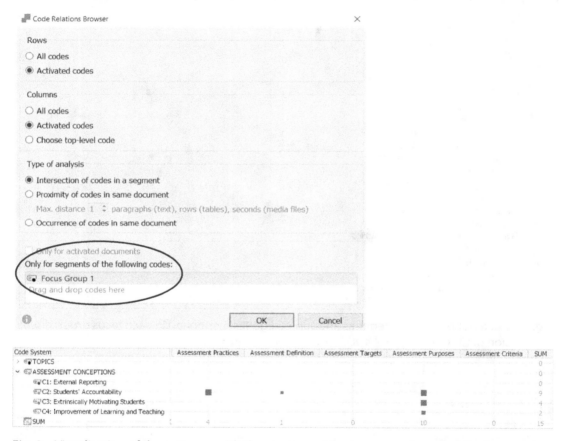

Fig. 9: Visualization of the category with the most consistent presence in one of the focus groups of Class A using MAXQDA's Code Relation Browser features

3.4 Summarizing and writing

MAXQDA's visual tools gave us considerable information about how elementary Portuguese teachers and students perceived assessment in mathematics and about the similarities and disparities that emerge when students' and teachers' conceptions were compared. Therefore, we developed a strategy to organize and write our results using the Summary Grid and Summary Tables.

We used the Summary Grid (**Analysis > Summary Grid**) to organize our findings. With this tool, we could create thematic summaries for each document (displayed in the grid as columns) about the categories in the analyses (displayed in the rows). Since writing summaries can take a long time, we chose to summarize, for each document, only the categories most often covered (visualized with the Document Portrait), the categories broken down into the maximum number of aspects (visualized with the Code Matrix Browser), and the categories mentioned in (nearly) all the interview topics (visualized with the Code Relations Browser). Since the Summary Grid displayed the corresponding code segments of the category in analyses in the middle window, we were always close to the data it summarized, making it easy to check our conclusions and to include translated quotes into a summary. We also included some ideas about why there were similarities or differences between teachers' and students' conceptions, and how we could test these hypotheses in future studies.

After writing all summaries, we created a Summary Table with all our cases for systematic case comparisons and contrast. This is easily done by clicking on the icon **Summary Table** in the Summary Grid window. In this table, all associated summaries are displayed together. We displayed our cases (documents) in the columns (teacher and students on the same class side by side) and the *Assessment Conceptions* categories in the row. We inspected all categories and compared each teacher's discourse with their students' discourse (within-case analysis). We also conducted a cross-case analysis to deepen our understanding of the phenomenon (Miles et al., 2014). We wrote down our conclusion in a Microsoft Word document, including quotes and excerpts that demonstrated our findings. The process was straightforward because summaries are linked to the coded segments of interest.

Briefly, our results indicated some inconsistency between students' and teachers' assessment conceptions. If we ordered our participants along the continuum ranging from the assessment OF learning pole (AoL) to the assessment FOR learning pole (AfL) (Fig. 10), most of the students seemed to be predominantly at the AoL pole of the continuum, while most of the teachers were at the AfL pole. Only for Class A were the teacher's and students' conceptions of assessment aligned. In Class E, we also observed some similarities, but in the majority of classes, the teacher's and students' assessment conceptions were not aligned. We believe that this disparity may be due to inconsistencies between teachers' conceptions and assessment practices. We hope to deepen this issue in future studies.

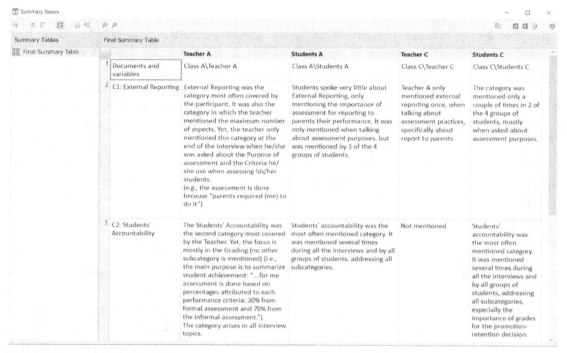

Fig. 10: Excerpt of the final Summary Table

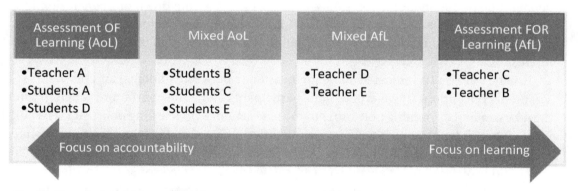

Fig. 11: Description of the comprehensive conceptions of teachers and students

4   Lessons learned

This chapter detailed a case study with both single-person and focus group interviews conducted in the field of educational research. We hope that our explicit descriptions provide guidance and inspiration to researchers who wish to use MAXQDA not only to study individual cases but also for comparing cases. We illustrated several practical aspects of the analyses, such as possible strategies for organizing the data, developing a code system, visualizing and summarizing data, and writing findings. Moreover, it is important to highlight the following for those considering comparing single-person and focus group interviews:

❖ Document organization: The way data are organized in the Document System affects whether we can directly compare two documents or two groups of documents in a single action. Because we were comparing teachers' and students' conceptions, we thought that maintaining all focus groups in one document would facilitate the comparison between the subjects. In fact, it did help. However, this raised some difficulties when assessing consistency within the focus group data. Another possibility is organizing the data of each focus group in one single document, and then storing all the focus group documents from the same class in a document group. Such organization allows for a more efficient review of the data for each focus group and most of the features of the MAXQDA allow comparisons between document groups, so it is still possible to compare all students' data with the teacher's data. The only feature that cannot be displayed for the document group is the Document Portrait. Still, it is possible to calculate the percentage of text covered for the document group with the Code Coverage feature. However, it is challenging to change the organization of the data after they become set as documents, so it is essential to decide how to organize the data before adding it to the MAXQDA project. Luckily, MAXQDA is very versatile, and "there will always be other ways to accomplish the same task" (Woolf & Silver, 2018, p. 73), even though less straightforward, as we demonstrated in this study case.

❖ Coding process: In our case study, we only demonstrated how we analyzed data at the group level. However, owing to the characteristics of focus group discussions, it is possible to analyze the data at the participant level. MAXQDA can simplify the process of importing focus group transcripts that can be coded automatically with structural codes with the name of the focus group and sub-codes with the name of participants (see Kuckartz & Rädiker, 2019, pp. 203–205). These codes will allow for the analysis of each participants' contributions.

❖ Analysis process: We analyzed our data using standard analysis methods for qualitative interviews. However, there are special techniques developed for group analyses, and there are several functions in MAXQDA that were developed specifically for this form of data. We recommend exploring these functions in Kuckartz and Rädiker (2019).

We hope that these recommendations will help and inspire other researchers who are conducting similar analyses and experience similar issues.

Bibliography

Andersson, N. (2016). Teacher's conceptions of quality in dance education expressed through grade conferences. *Journal of Pedagogy, 7*(2), 11–32. https://doi.org/10.1515/jped-2016-0014

Azis, A. (2015). Conceptions and practices of assessment: A case of teachers representing improvement conception. *TEFLIN Journal, 26*(2), 129–154. https://doi.org/10.15639/teflinjournal.v26i2/129–154

Bengtsson, M. (2016). How to plan and perform a qualitative study using content analysis. *NursingPlus Open, 2*, 8–14. http://dx.doi.org/10.1016/j.npls.2016.01.001

Brinkmann, S. (2013). *Qualitative interviewing.* Oxford.

Brown, G. T. L. (2008). *Conceptions of assessment: Understanding what assessment means to teachers and students.* Nova Science Publishers.

Brown, G. T. L. (2013). *Conceptions of assessment. Understanding what assessment means to teachers and students.* Nova Science Publishers.

Brown, G. T. L. (2018). *Assessment of student achievement.* Routledge.

Carless, D. (2009). Learning-oriented assessment: Principles, practice, and a project. In L. H. Meyer, S. Davidson, H. Anderson, R. Fletcher, P. M. Johnston, & M. Rees (Eds.), *Tertiary assessment and higher education student outcomes: Policy, practice, and research* (pp. 79–90). Wellington, NZ: Ako Aotearoa & Victoria University of Wellington

Chmiliar, L. (2012). Multiple-case designs. In A. J. Mills, G. Durepos, & E. Wiebe (Eds.), *Encyclopedia of case study research* (pp. 583–584). Sage. https://doi.org/10.4135/9781412957397.n216

Creswell, J. W., & Poth, C. N. (2018). *Qualitative inquiry and research design: Choosing among five approaches.* Sage.

Gipps, C. (1999). Socio-cultural aspects of assessment. *Review of Research in Education, 24*, 355–392. https://doi.org/10.3102/0091732X024001355

Guest, G., Namey, E. E., & Mitchell, M. L. (2013). *Collecting qualitative data. A field manual for applied research.* Sage.

Kuckartz, U., & Rädiker, S. (2019). *Analyzing qualitative data with MAXQDA. Text, audio, and video* Springer Nature Switzerland. https://doi.org/10.1007/978-3-030-15671-8

Miles, M. B., Huberman, A. M., & Saldaña, J. (2014). *Qualitative data analysis: A methods sourcebook* (3rd ed.). Sage.

Remesal, A. (2006). *Los problemas en la evaluación del aprendizaje matemático en la educación obligatoria: perspectiva de profesores y alumnos* [Problems in the evaluation of mathematical learning in compulsory education: Perspectives of teachers and students] (Doctoral Thesis). Universitat de Barcelona, Departament de Psicologia Evolutiva i de l'Educació, Barcelona.

Saldaña, J. (2013). *The coding manual for qualitative researchers.* Sage.

Woolf, N. H., & Silver, C. (2018). *Qualitative analysis using MAXQDA: The five level QDA method.* Routledge.

About the authors

Natalie Nóbrega Santos is a PhD student at the ISPA – Instituto Universitário, where she is also lecturing Research Methodology for Kindergarten and Elementary School Teachers. Her research interest fields are academic assessment, the affective components of achievement, grade retention, and social and emotional learning
ORCID: https://orcid.org/0000-0002-4973-9311

Vera Monteiro graduated in Educational Psychology at the ISPA – Instituto Universitário and has a PhD in the same domain by the University of Lisbon. She has been a professor at ISPA-Instituto Universitário since 1991. Her research interests are assessment and feedback and their relation to learning through affective processes, such as motivation, engagement, self-perception competence, and/or through several different cognitive processes.
ORCID: https://orcid.org/0000-0002-4250-7040

Lourdes Mata is an Assistant Professor at the ISPA – Instituto Universitário. She graduated in Educational Psychology and has a PhD in Children's Studies by the Universidade do Minho. She studies the affective components of the learning processes, aiming to identify and characterize individual beliefs and affective learning facets among students throughout schooling.
ORCID: https://orcid.org/0000-0001-8645-246X

This study was supported by the FCT – Science and Technology Foundation – Research project PTDC/MHC-CED/1680/2014 and UID/CED/04853/2016.

Using MAXQDA's Visual Tools:
An Example with Historical Legal Documents

Andreas W. Müller

Abstract

To analyze process-generated data, like court records, protocols, media reports, or forms, MAXQDA and especially its visual tools are useful to investigate their internal structure. This chapter illustrates how court records from the 16th and 17th century were analyzed using the Compare Group function, Code Matrix Browser, Document Comparison Chart, and the Code Relations Browser. By using consistent analytical units that reflect the internal structure of the documents and by utilizing code colors, structures within the data emerge that have major implications for studying their creation and use. In this example, the Compare Group function highlighted differences between the two analytical groups. The Code Matrix Browser was used to investigate the changes of subject along the temporal sequence of the documents. The Document Comparison Chart allowed me to analyze the practices of the two courts by analyzing their rigor and consistency in the subjects they cover. Finally, the Code Relations Browser provided insights into the internal consistency and usage differences of the concept-driven code system.

Key MAXQDA features covered

- ✓ Document Variables
- ✓ Compare Cases & Groups (Quantitative)
- ✓ Code Matrix Browser
- ✓ Code Relations Browser
- ✓ Document Comparison Chart

1   Introduction

The data at the heart of this analysis is not a very recent one. In fact, it was written 400 years ago. Still it can be effective in demonstrating a general methodological challenge: how to analyze process-generated data with the help of visual tools. Unlike interviews or surveys, the umbrella term "process-generated data" (compare Bauernschmidt, 2014, p. 418) covers all research data that is not created with a scientific research interest in mind. Instead, the researcher is faced with data that was created out of a practical purpose. Instead of carefully controlling the data creation, the researcher is often unfamiliar with the material that is already in final form and cannot be influenced or changed. The analyst here must make the best of the material available. For analyzing such data, visuals tools can be the researcher's best ally because they allow to unveil thematic structures that provide insights into the usage and circumstances of the creation of the data. Overall, this use case demonstrates how MAXQDA and especially its visual tools can be useful to analyze process-generated data and what precautions must be considered before setting up the analysis.

The data analyzed here are both: strongly structured and unfamiliar to anyone living in the 21st century. As court records, they are the product of a process of varying formality. The result of these legal processes comes by and large out of a black box. Researchers know the general proceedings of early modern courts but in most cases cannot trace the individual people, customs and decisions that caused the final form of the material (Voltmer, 2015, pp. 30–33).

The documents analyzed here are summarized "confessions protocols." This type of document is called "Urgicht" by contemporaries and summarizes the final deeds that the accused (supposedly) admitted (Dillinger, 2007, p. 193). They were created during witchcraft trials in Rostock (Germany, 1584) and Hainburg (Austria, 1617–18). The aim of the research was to apply a theoretical model of witchcraft belief, created by theologians in the early modern period and reconstructed by historians today. Do these two distant places follow the doctrinal teachings of their time? Do they use shared ideas and concepts of witchcraft? What unique local elements do they incorporate? Such were the research questions that were largely answered with the help of MAXQDA. In this paper the methods and the software side of the research are presented. The relevant findings for historical research have been published in detail in Müller (2019).

2   Data collection and methodological approach

The data set collected here consists of 37 "confession protocols," 19 created in 1617–18 in Hainburg and 18 in Rostock in 1584. These two groups will be compared throughout the analysis. The original documents reside in archives in Lower Austria and Mecklenburg. Transcripts of the (cursive) handwriting were created to import them as plain text documents into MAXQDA.

A key feature of these documents is their clear (although not always concise) structure. Each document is structured with numbered paragraphs starting with the same initial word "Bekennt / Admits...." (Fig. 1). Although the amount and contents of these paragraphs vary from document to document, this internal structure was of key importance for the analysis. Each paragraph was taken as an analytical unit to allow for quantitative analysis and structural comparison.

As the goal of the research was to utilize and test a pre-existing concept of witchcraft, a concept-driven approach was chosen. Historians have recreated the early modern theological idea of witchcraft to consist of five main aspects:

- ❖ Pact with the devil
- ❖ Intercourse with the devil
- ❖ Magical flight
- ❖ Witches' gathering
- ❖ Harmful magic

These five aspects are well-known and commonly used in the literature as the "elaborated concept of witchcraft" (Behringer, 1997, p. 15, 2004, p. 57; Dillinger, 2007, p. 21; Goodare, 2016, p. 76; Lorenz, 2004, p. 131). In this analysis the five aspects served as the concept-driven code system applied to the material. For a more detailed analysis the category of "harmful magic" was subdivided by creating data-driven, inductive sub-categories (Mayring, 2015, pp. 97–109). In several iterations of coding, each paragraph of the transcripts was coded with one or several of the five categories (if applicable). Thus, the content was structured along specific themes based on the literature.

3   Analysis with Visual Tools

After importing the data, the 37 text documents were split into two document groups ("Hainburg 1617/18" and "Rostock 1584") for comparison in the later analysis (Fig. 1). The documents were provided with an ID reflecting their chronological order, which proved to be of key importance for the later analysis. In this way, whenever documents are sorted by name, they already allow insights into changes along the chronology of the two one-year mass trials.

The deductive categories were defined using the code memo function. Furthermore, each category received a unique color that can be easily remembered (like black for black magic, red for the devil's pact, etc.) which enables the use of more advanced visual tools.

When reading and coding the documents, Document Variables were created, and values gathered. Throughout the process of coding, metadata was gathered such as gender, age, date, use of torture, verdict, etc. As each document reflects one person, the document variables could be used as biographical data. Gathering this structured metadata allowed for detailed analysis of subgroups by using Activate Documents by Variable or Crosstab (both available in the **Mixed Methods** menu). In this way, tortured and not-tortured persons, men and women, executed and not-executed people could be compared. This proved of great value beyond the use of visual tools demonstrated here.

Furthermore, document memos were used to write short summaries, take notes, and record further metadata on each case. This allowed to quickly identify the documents and to summarize their uniqueness or commonalities. Also, MAXMaps was used to provide a visual overview of the different steps within the trials and the accusations going back and forth between the accused.

However, at the center of the analysis stood four analytical tools: the Compare Group function, the Code Matrix Browser, the Document Comparison Chart and the Code Relations Browser.

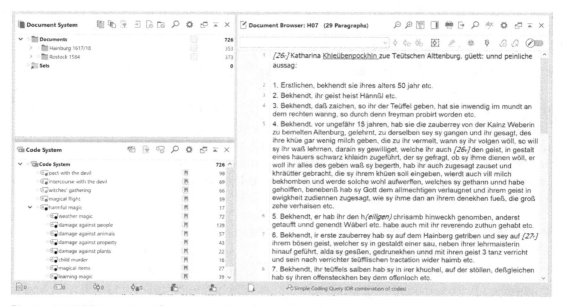

Fig. 1: MAXQDA project after completing the coding phase

3.1 Frequency analysis with Compare Groups

After working through the material three times, each paragraph was coded with one or several of the five categories (if applicable). Because most visualizations reflect numerical values in some way, this step needed special caution.

As the goal of the analysis was to compare the two trials in relation to their conception of witchcraft, the first simple step was to compare the two document groups by using the quantitative Compare Cases & Groups feature (**Analysis > Compare Cases & Groups > Quantitative**) which creates a crosstab that allows for both a quantitative and also visual interpretation by using the background coloring option.

Fig. 2 shows absolute values with clear differences between the groups. Several noticeable patterns came up and reflect a different emphasis on individual elements of the witchcraft accusation.

	Rostock 1584	Hainburg 1617/18	Total
pact with the devil	27	71	98
intercourse with the devil	40	29	69
witches' gathering	22	44	66
magical flight	16	43	59
harmful magic	1	16	17
weather magic	7	65	72
damage against people	120	19	139
damage against animals	46	11	57
damage against property	41	2	43
damage against plants		22	22
child murder	9	9	18
magical items	20	7	27
learning magic	24	15	39
Σ SUM	373	353	726
# N = Documents	18 (48.6%)	19 (51.4%)	37 (100.0%)

Fig. 2: Compare groups, absolute numbers of coded segments

In this project, the number of coded segments in the compared groups was almost identical (373 to 353) and likewise the number of documents were close (18 to 19). If the two groups had differed more regarding the number of documents and coded segments, using percentages might become an important step. In Fig. 3, the tendency does not change much when percentages per column are chosen to even out the different number of paragraphs between the groups.

	Rostock 1584	Hainburg 1617/18	Total
pact with the devil	7.2%	20.1%	13.5%
intercourse with the devil	10.7%	8.2%	9.5%
witches' gathering	5.9%	12.5%	9.1%
magical flight	4.3%	12.2%	8.1%
harmful magic	0.3%	4.5%	2.3%
weather magic	1.9%	18.4%	9.9%
damage against people	32.2%	5.4%	19.1%
damage against animals	12.3%	3.1%	7.9%
damage against property	11.0%	0.6%	5.9%
damage against plants		6.2%	3.0%
child murder	2.4%	2.5%	2.5%
magical items	5.4%	2.0%	3.7%
learning magic	6.4%	4.2%	5.4%
Σ SUM	100.0%	100.0%	100.0%
# N = Documents	18 (48.6%)	19 (51.4%)	37 (100.0%)

Fig. 3: Compare groups, relative numbers

To elaborate only on one example, in Hainburg, a small town in a wine growing region transforming the weather by spells was the most frequently reported instance of "black magic" (65 paragraphs). Not only did the destruction of crops and wine during the so-called "Little Ice Age" (Behringer, 1991, p. 339) cause great mischief for the people, but also the idea of the weather making witch was more prominent in Catholicism. In contrast, this category is almost nonexistent in Rostock, where trade and growing hop and barley was less vulnerable to weather and theological ideas regarded influencing the weather as superstition. Instead, causing damage against people, such as spreading sickness and causing accidents, was the dominant deed reported in the large town of Rostock.

Here the Compare Group function utilizes the internal structure of the process-generated data and shows some broad stroke differences between groups of the material. In this analysis, both groups were of a similar size and length. The segment was in itself meaningful. However, in other cases it is more important to think closely about the size of coded segments. If there is no consistent meaning attributed to each segment, one is often forced to binarizing the frequency based on the number of documents (by clicking on the icon **Count hits only once per document** # in the toolbar). In this case, each document would only be counted once. As Fig. 4 shows, this would have blurred most of the more nuanced findings.

	Rostock 1584	Hainburg 1617/18	Total
pact with the devil	18	19	37
intercourse with the devil	17	18	35
witches' gathering	18	18	36
magical flight	16	18	34
harmful magic	1	13	14
weather magic	4	16	20
damage against people	18	8	26
damage against animals	14	10	24
damage against property	14	2	16
damage against plants		14	14
child murder	4	5	9
magical items	18	5	23
learning magic	18	15	33
Σ SUM	160	161	321
# N = Documents	18 (48.6%)	19 (51.4%)	37 (100.0%)

Fig. 4:   Compare groups, count coded segments from each document once only

Here, the difference in weather magic is still visible, as most documents in Rostock do not treat weather magic at all. However, the strong emphasis put on the pact of the devil in Hainburg becomes completely invisible. The pact was mentioned in all documents in Rostock at least once, but in Hainburg it was elaborated for many dozens of paragraphs. This effect only becomes visible when total numbers of meaningful segments are considered.

By having gathered document variables throughout the process, the researcher is not limited to contrasting document groups. In fact, a table just like the above can be created based on any document variable. For example, one could contrast the very unevenly large groups of people tortured and not-tortured in this sample (Fig. 5).

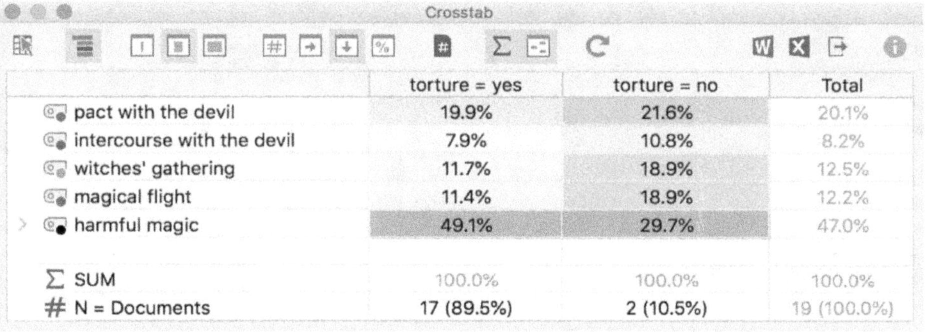

	torture = yes	torture = no	Total
pact with the devil	19.9%	21.6%	20.1%
intercourse with the devil	7.9%	10.8%	8.2%
witches' gathering	11.7%	18.9%	12.5%
magical flight	11.4%	18.9%	12.2%
harmful magic	49.1%	29.7%	47.0%
Σ SUM	100.0%	100.0%	100.0%
# N = Documents	17 (89.5%)	2 (10.5%)	19 (100.0%)

Fig. 5: Compare groups by document variable "torture" in a crosstab

Although only 2 of 19 people in Hainburg were not tortured and instead confessed quickly to escape the pains of interrogation, we can compare the percentages of these two with the rest of the sample. As Fig. 5 shows, we see that the confession without torture focused far less on harmful magic (30% compared to 49%). This indicated that the court was less interested in black magic compared to the diabolic elements of the pact, intercourse, gathering and flight. Again, if one would only look at binarized values per document, no effect at all would be visible as these five broad categories come up one way or another in each document.

We can see therefore when intending to analyze code frequencies (with whatever tool) it is of crucial importance to think beforehand what each segment is reflecting. If one cannot attribute meaning and consistency to each segment, the analytical options will be limited. When analyzing process-generated data an internal structure often exists. Paragraphs in legal texts, numbers of articles in a newspaper, or numbers of speeches in parliamentary debates, they all can be meaningfully quantified and be analyzed with the Compare Group, Code Matrix, and Cross Table function.

3.2 Distribution analysis with Code Matrix Browser

So far, only cumulative values for groups of documents were considered. However, as document IDs were applied following the chronological sequence of the documents, the code frequencies of the Code Matrix Browser (available in the **Visual Tools** menu) can be used to get longitudinal insights in the changes of topic over time. Each of the two mass trials lasted for roughly a year from the first accusation of a person to the execution of the last. In this way one can investigate different stages of the trials and compare them based on the topics that appear.

Code System	H01	H02	H03	H04	H05	H06	H07	H08	H09	H10	H11	H12	H13	H14	H15	H16	H17	H18	H19	SUM
pact with the devil																				71
intercourse with the devil																				29
witches' gathering																				44
magical flight																				43
harmful magic																				15
weather magic																				65
damage against people																				19
damage against animals																				11
damage against property																				2
damage against plants																				22
child murder																				9
magical items																				7
learning magic																				15
Σ SUM	23	12	27	1	14	15	27	17	26	34	21	19	20	19	12	15	17	16	18	353

Fig. 6: Code Matrix Browser, Hainburg

Fig. 6 shows the Code Matrix Browser for the documents of Hainburg. Now, instead of each column representing a group, each column represents an individual document. The number of H01 to H19 follows the sequence of the trials. The size of each square reflects the frequency of this code in the respective document. Because the individual documents vary in length, I chose the option to calculate the size of the symbols based on the column to correct for that. In relation to the absolute number of segments, the observed effect would remain the same, however shorter documents would become less visible. In Fig. 6, we see that weather magic was much more prominent in documents H05 to H12. Also, we see that the first document H01 is much more diverse in topics.

Manually adding some lines in an image editing software between the three stages of the trial (1st, 2nd, and 3rd wave), the pattern becomes even more pronounced. As Fig. 7 shows, in the early stage of the trial, the accusations were more "individual." In the second stage from H05 to H12 a strong emphasis on bad weather (maybe due to recent events) influenced the trials. In the third stage, black magic became less prominent in general, as shorter trials only focused on the more diabolic issues such as pact and intercourse with the devil or the witches' gathering and flight.

Code System	H01	H02	H03	H04	H05	H06	H07	H08	H09	H10	H11	H12	H13	H14	H15	H16	H17	H18	H19	SUM
harmful magic																				15
weather magic																				65
damage against people																				19
damage against animals																				11
damage against property																				2
damage against plants																				22
child murder																				9
magical items																				7
learning magic																				15

Fig. 7: Code Matrix Browser, Hainburg. Trial stages separated by lines

Looking at the same overview for Rostock in Fig. 8, no such clear stages exist. However, a clear change in the pattern from document R09 to R12 occurs. There, the focus shifts from damage against people to damage against animals. This shifting pattern led to a follow up investigation. First, I checked the document variables for commonalities that might help to explain this shift. Here, I noticed that all four accused came not from Rostock itself but from the small village of "Warnemünde" near the town of Rostock. Closely rereading the statements with a focus on the socio-economic life of the accused brought to light that they were herders from the countryside, not beggers in the streets. Thus, they are more frequently connected to causing sickness or death among livestock.

Code System	R01	R02	R03	R04	R05	R06	R07	R08	R09	R10	R11	R12	R13	R14	R15	R16	R17	R18	SUM
pact with the devil																			27
intercourse with the devil																			40
witches' gathering																			22
magical flight																			16
harmful magic																			1
weather magic																			7
damage against people																			120
damage against animals																			46
damage against property																			41
damage against plants																			0
child murder																			9
magical items																			20
learning magic																			24
Σ SUM	17	11	26	17	19	17	31	27	16	13	17	28	28	25	22	21	20	20	373

Fig. 8: Code Matrix Browser, Rostock

For interpretations such as these, again a meaningful size of the coded segment is key. With only binarized values per document, no clear pattern would become visible. This shows how a look at the distribution of code frequencies can help to identify or analyze different stages that process-generated data covers. For this it is necessary to think closely on how to name and sort the documents. Only by using document IDs that reflect the time sequence, temporal changes could have been made visible. A random order of the documents above would make it much more difficult to interpret the results. This analysis shows where patterns are followed and where individual differences occur. This can be particularly useful in tracing different influences on the data and understanding the mechanisms that created it.

As a follow up to this analysis, Document Sets could be created, representing the different stages of the trial and to compare them qualitatively or quantitatively with the Compare Groups function. In this way the visual tools not only allow to look at final results but also can inspire further research steps as they allow to identify patterns that can be investigated further.

3.3 Structural analysis with Document Comparison Chart

Continuing such a structural analysis, the level of detail can be broken down even further. Until now, groups of documents were considered, later individual documents followed. With the Document Comparison Chart (**Visual Tools > Document Comparison Chart**), one can continue to look at the distribution of codes within individual documents. When analyzing such clearly pre-structured process-generated material the Document Comparison Chart becomes a useful tool. It allows insights into the thematical structure of the analyzed documents. Where and in what sequence did different topics appear in the documents?

Besides using meaningful segments that reflect the internal structure of documents, one key requirement is the usage of code colors. Here, the major difficulty is to select the right variety of colors. Too many colors may prevent the meaningful interpretation of the data as the association between code and color becomes unclear. They can only become useful for the interpretation when the researcher can easily remember the meaning of each color and tell them apart. On the other hand, if too few colors are used important distinctions within the data might be lost. One critical step here is to limit the codes for the visualization via the Activate function. Only analyzing a handful of colors at the same time and varying the level of granularity has proven important here. For example, in Fig. 9 and Fig. 10 all five main categories received a unique and clearly distinct color (red, brown, blue, pink, black) that was also used for all sub-codes. Also, it helps to identify the codes with a color that somehow resembles the content. Here for example "black" for "black magic," red for the devil, or blue (like the sky) for flight were selected. Other codes of secondary interest were only added in later stages to investigate the gaps in the visual display of the material (Fig. 10). These gaps indicate portions of text that were not coded with any of the concept-driven codes. Coding such segments of text with data-driven codes allowed to explain in detail what elements outside of the "elaborated concept of witchcraft" still make it into the trial records.

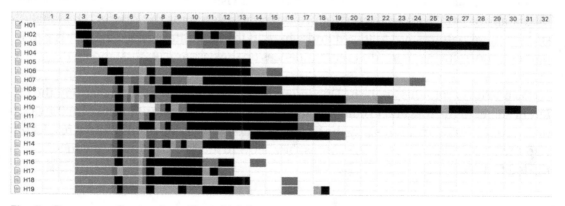

Fig. 9:   Document Comparison Chart, Hainburg

In Fig. 9, the 19 documents of the Hainburg trials can be seen. Each line represents one document and each column one of the numbered paragraphs: Paragraphs 3–6 are predominantly red, while paragraphs 7–9 are blue and pink, and from 10 onwards black is of great prominence. This shows that a structure was consistently followed in the creation of these documents. The documents all began with describing the meeting and alliance with the devil, afterwards went on describing the flight and meeting of the witches and lastly listed a varying number of evil magical deeds such as influencing the weather, harming crops, livestock, or humans. This visualization also draws attention to the changing length of the documents. Here, the variation in length is mainly made up by the varying detail on black magic. In some documents the list of magical deeds continued extensively (e.g., H01, H07, H10). Others ended quickly after the first four categories were briefly covered. In this case the individual variety of the documents lies not in the more "theological" elements of the pact of the devil but in how many or how few statements about magic were made. Here, individual statements were more likely to influence the subject, whereas the more firmly codified verdicts of the devil's pact and magical meetings are at least in quantity less impacted by the statements of the accused.

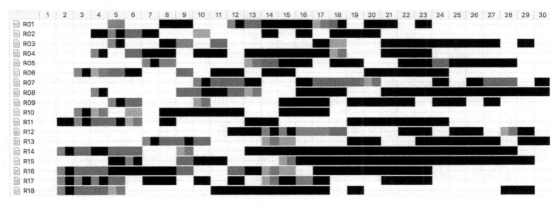

Fig. 10: Document Comparison Chart, Rostock (only first 30 paragraphs are displayed)

As a contrasting example, Fig. 10 shows the trials of Rostock. Here, the structure is less clear. Many gaps appear early in the material and the distribution of topics is less pronounced. The courts in Rostock apparently did not follow such a clear pattern as their counterparts in Hainburg. The contents were more flexible. However, the basic pattern red-blue/pink-black is still recognizable here. In fact, the pattern seems to be trans regional and be followed by both places. Here too, most documents start with the pact with the devil and move on to magical flights and meetings while ending on black magic. When filling in the gap by activating further codes created during the analysis, the differences between both places quickly become clear.

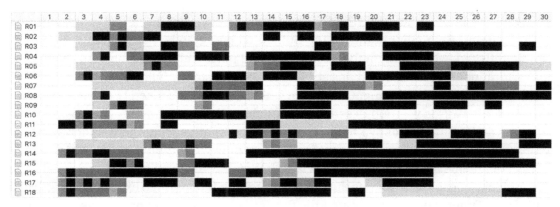

Fig. 11: Document Comparison Chart, Rostock with popular magic (only first 30 paragraphs are displayed)

Fig. 11 shows a yellow code that represents non-harmful magic use such as fortune telling or healing, which fills in many of the gaps. Whereas in Hainburg all magic was by definition diabolic and harmful, in Rostock positive magic attempts (considered as superstition or fraud) were considered to exist without the immediate influence of the devil. Several documents (R01, R02, R03, R05, R07, R12, R13) start with non-maleficent magic use and more resemble a two-part structure of non-harmful and harmful magic use intersected by the meeting with the devil.

In many contexts, such structural analysis and comparison can be of great use especially for process-generated data. However, the Document Comparison Chart here does not only severe as a tool for the presentation of results, instead it can be used as a roadmap into once own data. Each of the cells above can be used to navigate into the specific document right away. If the gap in R01, paragraph 6, needs investigation, one click opens the corresponding section in the Document Browser.

Furthermore, this visual overview can provide similar insights as the Code Coverage analysis. One look at the Document Comparison Chart and the researcher will immediately be reminded how much data was coded in comparison with the total material. Especially during inductive category formation, this can be an important reminder and in times quite humbling when one is reminded of how little of the data most of the interpretations are built on.

3.4 Co-occurrence analysis with Code Relations Browser

So far, different ways to analyze the structure of the documents have been shown. However, by looking at code co-occurrence visualized with the Code Relations Browser, an evaluation of the code system and the integrity of the underlying concepts can be made. Each of the paragraphs in this analysis received one or several of the five concept-driven categories. With this non-exclusive coding strategy, I was able to take a look at what topics appear together in each paragraph.

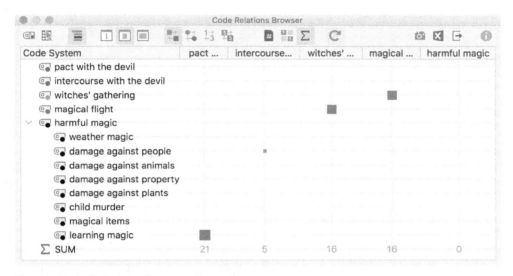

Fig. 12: Code Relations Browser, Rostock

In Fig. 12, the Code Relations Browser (available in the **Visual Tools** menu) for Rostock is shown. The size of the icons reflects how frequently each code co-occurs with another code at the same text segment (paragraph). Here, we see 16 co-occurrences of the witches' flight and gathering as well as 21 of learning of magic and the devil's pact. Both combinations narratively often appear together. Damage against people and intercourse with the devil highlights five narratives where the jealous devil is taking action against the witch's husband.

More interesting than these clear-cut co-occurrences in Rostock is the much greater richness in code-co-occurrences in Hainburg (Fig. 13). Here, various combinations exist frequently. Although the length and level of detail of each paragraph is similar in both data sets, the patterns observed here are strongly different. In Hainburg, all kinds of witchcraft elements are described together and reflect a well-integrated set of beliefs. For example, the magical flight co-occurs with other codes at 48 segments. The flight's details are discussed, locations mentioned, and various spells conjured in the air. In Rostock, on contrast, the witches flight exclusively occurs whenever there is a gathering. In all other deeds or daily narratives this element is completely absent from the trial records. This is a strong indicator that at the protestant court of Rostock the magical flight was a rather unfamiliar element that was only needed to explain the gatherings. Likely the flights were interpreted as dreams and not considered an essential set of a witch's powers.

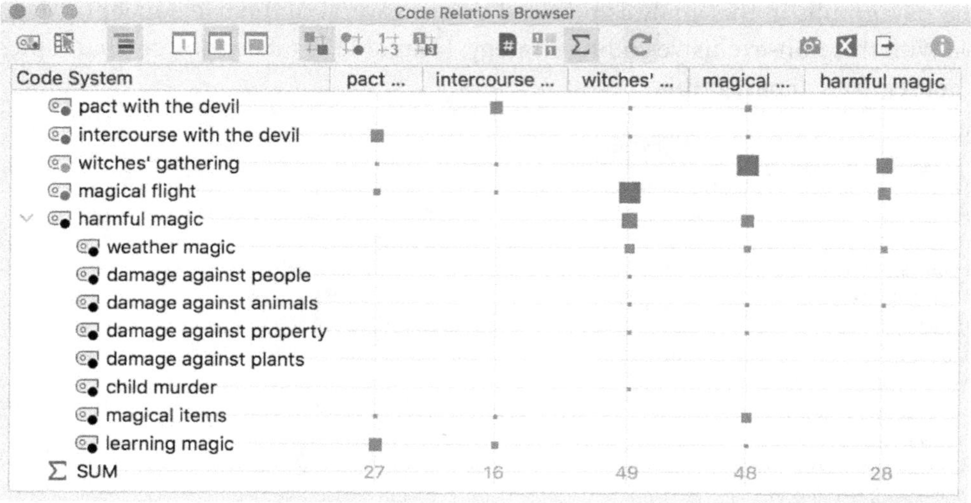

Code System	pact ...	intercourse ...	witches' ...	magical ...	harmful magic
pact with the devil		■	·	■	
intercourse with the devil	■		·	·	
witches' gathering	·	·		■	■
magical flight	·	·	■		■
harmful magic			■	■	
weather magic			■	·	·
damage against people			·		
damage against animals			·	·	·
damage against property			·	·	
damage against plants			·	·	
child murder			·		
magical items	·	·		■	
learning magic	■	■		·	
∑ SUM	27	16	49	48	28

Fig. 13: Code Relations Browser, Hainburg

By analyzing code co-occurrences, relationships between concept-driven categories can be explored in detail. Here, it became possible to identify more "foreign" or isolated elements within the data. Using consistent analytical units and clear coding rules is again key. Furthermore, it is important that the level of detail remains consistent throughout most of the material. If some segments are detailed descriptions and others remain general this could blur the analysis as co-occurrences become more likely in more detailed or extensive sections of text. In this analysis, the findings with Code Relations Browser can be supported by the qualitative impression of the researcher and be well explained when consulting research literature. Overall, this analysis proved highly useful as it highlighted tendencies in the material that would likely have passed the eye of the researcher without the many analysis options of MAXQDA.

4 Lessons learned

MAXQDA can be useful for identifying patterns in process-generated data. Whether they are reports in the media, protocols from political events, records from administrations, e-mail or letter correspondence or even archival data, MAXQDA can help to identify patterns of topics and to investigate the potential connections and external influences causing regularity or irregularities. Analyzing frequencies, distributions, structure, and code co-occurrence can inspire, enlighten, and reinforce qualitative research.

However, analyzing such data comes with specific requirements to maximize the output of the analysis. This use case demonstrated here shows how important it is to carefully consider the analytical units for this type of analysis. A meaningful quantification of the data is only possible when the units of analysis consistently reflect the internal structure of the documents. Furthermore, the careful choice of code colors is necessary to balance between too much noise and a unicolor image. When strategies of analysis and data visualization are known beforehand, coded segments can be applied in a way to support the analysis tools that will later be used.

Overall, creating stunning visual results with MAXQDA is often just a question of a few clicks. However, interpreting and validating these results is the key challenge of any researcher. Here, the data must be known and understood very well. Each occurring pattern must be critically considered as a false positive. For example, differences in code frequency can reflect a different length in document or amount of coded segments (as observed in 3.1), shifting topics over time (as observed in 3.2.) could easily reflect the analyst's behavior in dealing with an unstable and still evolving code system. Strong contrasts of code co-occurrence (as observed in 3.4) can be based on changing levels of detail. Therefore, it is important to be transparent about the research process. A clear research question and strategy are important, instead of just pushing buttons until any interesting result comes up.

In this, this use case shows the importance of an adequate training in the software and the related methodologies before undertaking any major research project. With pilot studies, adequate training, and a clear research plan in mind, exploring the labyrinth of data can turn into following a clear road on a fruitful research journey.

Bibliography

Bauernschmidt, S. (2014). Kulturwissenschaftliche Inhaltsanalyse prozessgenerierter Daten. In C. Bischoff, K. Oehme-Jüngling, & Leimgruber (Eds.), *UTB Kulturwissenschaft: Vol. 3948. Methoden der Kulturanthropologie* (pp. 415–430). Haupt Verlag.

Behringer, W. (1991). Climatic change and witch-hunting: The impact of the Little Ice Age on mentalities. *Climatic Change, 43*, 335–351. https://doi.org/10.1023/A:1005554519604

Behringer, W. (1997). *Hexenverfolgung in Bayern: Volksmagie, Glaubenseifer und Staatsräson in der Frühen Neuzeit* (3rd ed.). R. Oldenbourg.

Behringer, W. (2004). *Witches and witch-hunts: A global history.* Polity Press.

Dillinger, J. (2007). *Hexen und Magie: Eine historische Einführung.* Campus Verlag.

Goodare, J. (2016). *The European witch-hunt.* Routledge.

Kuckartz, U. (2014). *Mixed Methods: Methodologie, Forschungsdesigns und Analyseverfahren.* Springer VS. https://doi.org/10.1007/978-3-531-93267-5

Lorenz, S. (2004). Der Hexenprozess. In S. Lorenz (Ed.), *Wider alle Hexerei und Teufelswerk: Die Europäische Hexenverfolgung und ihre Auswirkungen auf Südwestdeutschland* (pp. 131–154). Thorbecke.

Mayring, P. (2015). *Qualitative Inhaltsanalyse: Grundlagen und Techniken* (12. ed.). Beltz Juventa.

Müller, A. (2019). Elaborated concepts of witchcraft? Applying the "elaborated concept of witchcraft" in a comparative study on the witchcraft trials of Rostock (1584) and Hainburg (1617–18). *E-Rhizome*, *1*(1), 1–22. https://doi.org/10.5507/rh.2019.001

Voltmer, R. (2015). Stimmen der Frauen? Gerichtsakten und Gender Studies am Beispiel der Hexenforschung. In J. Blume, J. Moos, & A. Conrad (Eds.), *Frauen, Männer, Queer: Ansätze und Perspektiven aus der historischen Genderforschung* (pp. 19–46). Röhrig Universitätsverlag.

About the author

Andreas W. Müller is an independent QDA trainer and commercial researcher working for projects in healthcare, education, and economics. Furthermore, he is a PhD candidate at the Martin-Luther University Halle/Wittenberg at the department of History. He has used MAXQDA since 2015 in a wide variety of research and teaching contexts.

ORCID: https://orcid.org/0000-0003-4603-5770

Twitter: https://twitter.com/aw_mueller

Using MAXQDA from Literature Review to Analyzing Coded Data: Following a Systematic Process in Student Research

Michael C. Gizzi, Alena Harm

Abstract

MAXQDA is a powerful tool for researchers of all levels, from undergraduates to doctoral students to seasoned researchers. With an organized structure to guide new users, MAXQDA can be easily used in undergraduate research. This chapter provides a case study of a student-driven research project showing how MAXQDA was used in a systematic way from crafting a literature review to developing a coding system and then to analyzing coded data. The research project showcased is focused on a legal research project in an undergraduate criminal justice course, which examines how lower courts interpret and comply with a U.S. Supreme Court decision. MAXQDA was used for the entire project, including conducting a literature review, paraphrasing cases to develop a coding system, and analyzing coded data. Code Frequencies were used to get an overview of the categorized crimes, the Code Relations Browser made it possible to look for code combinations, and Summary Tables were used to provide concise summaries of specific code usage.

Key MAXQDA features covered

- ✓ Paraphrasing
- ✓ Coding
- ✓ Document Variables
- ✓ Code Frequencies
- ✓ Code Relations Browser
- ✓ Code Matrix Browser
- ✓ Smart Coding Tool
- ✓ Word Cloud
- ✓ Summary Grid and Tables

1 Introduction

Student research using MAXQDA can seem overwhelming at first glance, given the wide range of tools available in the software, and no clear process of where to begin in a project, and once cases are coded, how to structure an analysis of the data. This chapter provides an example of a research project that was conducted by undergraduates and is intended to suggest a workflow that can be easily modified by others in conducting research across different disciplines.

The students in this project were new to MAXQDA and learned how to use the software in a stepwise learning approach, in which we only taught the tools necessary to accomplish each task. For example, in the beginning, we introduced MAXQDA to students using examples from other projects. And then proceeded to discuss the systematic approach we would take in this project, beginning with writing a literature review using MAXQDA to develop our research questions, exploring the documents using paraphrasing to develop a codebook, coding the data, and then analyzing the data with a focus on visual tools. We only discussed how to use the specific tools we needed for each task as we were completing that step in the process. It was a form of "just-in-time" training which was quite effective.

The student research project was focused on the judicial impact of a United States Supreme Court decision, which explores the ways the lower courts implement and interpret judicial policies established by the Supreme Court (Canon & Johnson, 1988). In our case, we were examining a judicially created policy called the "third-party doctrine" (TPD), which allows law enforcement to seek information from third parties (banks, phone companies, internet service providers, etc.) without a search warrant. The third-party doctrine is based on the principle that when an individual conducts business with a business or organization, like a phone company or bank, they have no privacy interest in the transaction records of the user's business relationship. And as a result, they cannot make a claim to be protected under the Fourth Amendment to the U.S. Constitution against "unreasonable searches and seizures" and government actors are not required to seek a warrant.

The third-party doctrine developed in a series of cases in the 1970s (*United States v. Miller*, 1976; *Smith v. Maryland*, 1979*)* and has been consistently been interpreted by lower courts as not requiring search warrants and has been used extensively by police as a way to gain evidence in criminal cases. Criticisms of the vast amount of discretion that the third-party doctrine provided law enforcement at the cost of individual rights and privacy has grown in the past decade (see, e.g., *United States v. Jones*, 2012).

In 2018, the Supreme Court decided a case that for the first time limited the government's ability to conduct warrantless searches under the third-party doctrine. *Carpenter v. United States* involved law enforcement requests to cell phone providers to provide "cell site location information" (CSLI) for specific phones. These records provided a detailed set of breadcrumbs providing information as to the location of a user's cell phone. The Supreme Court held that the privacy interests were so significant that the third-party doctrine would not be applied to this type of request. The Court's decision was seen as the first step in reconsidering the third-party doctrine.

A judicial impact study might appear to be a major undertaking for an undergraduate research project. MAXQDA offers the tools to minimize these concerns. Through a structured process, we were able to move the project from an idea to a complete analysis. This had several distinct steps:

- ❖ Literature review and development of specific research questions.
- ❖ Identification of data.
- ❖ Creation of a coding system and conducting a qualitative content analysis.
- ❖ Utilizing a structured process for analysis and writing results.

2   Literature review

In our study, we were interested in both the primary question of how case outcomes have changed as a result of the *Carpenter* decision and a broader question of better understanding the population of cases utilizing the third-party doctrine. We also wanted to know what types of criminal investigations involved third-party doctrine requests, and what types of third-party doctrine tools were used. We began the study with a literature review on the *Carpenter* decision and the third-party doctrine in general. We conducted searches in several academic databases, resulting in 14 articles from law review and popular media. Articles were downloaded as PDF files. News stories from websites were downloaded using the Google Chrome MAXQDA Web Collector extension.

A MAXQDA project was created for the literature review and the collected data was imported (**Import > Documents** and **Import > Web Collector Data**). This project file was used only for the review. The newspaper and magazine articles were stored in a separate document group to make it easier to distinguish them from the academic research (Fig. 1). Each article was read, and relevant parts of articles were paraphrased using MAXQDA's Paraphrase tool (**Analysis > Paraphrase Document**).

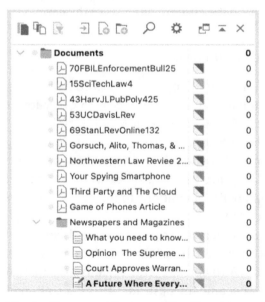

Fig. 1:   Document System of the literature review project

Once completed, we used the Paraphrases Matrix option (**Analysis > Paraphrase > Para-phrases Matrix**) to view each document's paraphrases in their entirety. The paraphrases were copied and pasted into a new document memo created for each article. The document memos became the equivalent of 3"x5" index cards for each article's notes. The document memos were then used to add in a written synopsis of the article's main points. In addition, when creating the document memos, we used five differently colored memo icons to distinguish between articles that focused on different aspects, such as technology or government efforts to invade privacy. Together the memos were used to write up the results of the literature review.

The literature review helped us to identify our final research questions, which were essential for the main part of the project:

❖ How have lower courts interpreted the *Carpenter* precedent, as it relates to other third-party doctrine issues, beyond cell phone tower logs (CSLI)?
❖ What surveillance tools do police use in third-party doctrine cases?
❖ What types of crimes do these cases involve?
❖ What legal doctrines have judges relied on in making their decision?
❖ To what degree have arguments made in *Carpenter* for potentially eliminating the third-party doctrine been referenced in lower court decisions?

3   Data collection and structuring the project file

With these questions to guide the study, we were ready to begin the main task of the research, developing a coding system, and conducting the content analysis of the cases.

3.1 Identifying, downloading, and importing documents

Data for this study came from a legal analysis citation tool known as *Shepard's Citations*, which is included within the *Lexis Uni* legal database. It provides access to every lower court decision that has either cited a case or provided analysis of it by either "following" the precedent or "distinguishing" the facts of the current case from the precedent being analyzed. We limited our dataset to cases that provided analysis and organized them into the two analytical types. The search results from *Shepards* can be easily downloaded as text files in numerous formats. We identified a complete list of citations to the case *Carpenter v. United States* from June 2018 until September 2020.

We narrowed the list to 236 cases from state and federal courts that provided "analysis" of *Carpenter,* either "following" the decision, or "distinguishing" the case from the precedent. Each case was downloaded in Microsoft Word format, and organized into two groups, "State Cases" and "Federal Cases." These became the basis for the organization of the documents in MAXQDA's Document System, where we created two similarly named document groups (Fig. 2).

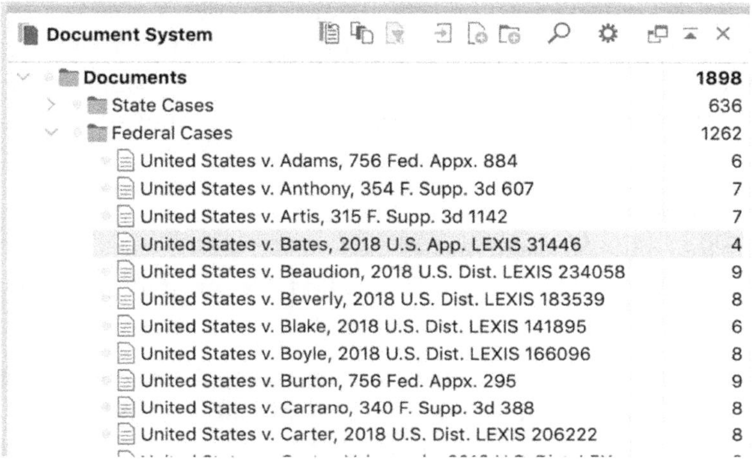

Fig. 2: Two document groups in the Document System for structuring the legal cases

3.2 Creating initial Document Variables

After organizing the documents by group, we created Document Variables for each case. First, we used **Variables > Export Document Variables** and opened the file in Microsoft Excel to create a clean and empty template for entering the variable values. We added several variables to the file, including year the case was decided, "Shepards" (to indicate how the case was characterized in the *Shepards* search), level of court (Federal or State), and type of court (appellate or trial). Once the spreadsheet was complete, we saved it and then used **Variables > Import Document Variables**, to include the new information in MAXQDA (Fig. 3).

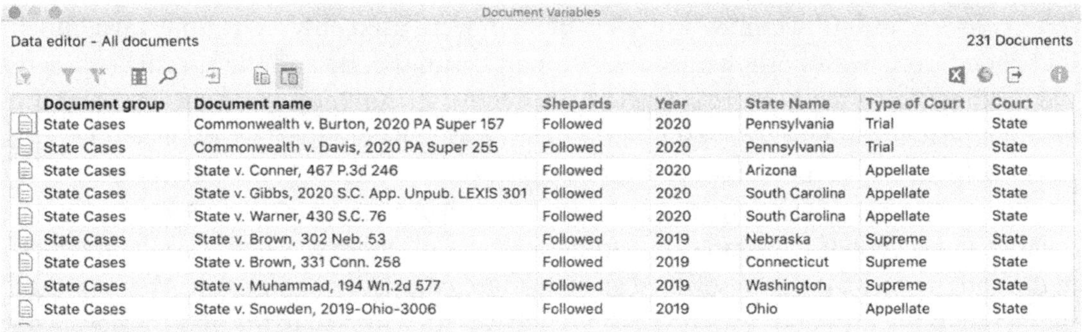
Document Variables

Data editor - All documents — 231 Documents

Document group	Document name	Shepards	Year	State Name	Type of Court	Court
State Cases	Commonwealth v. Burton, 2020 PA Super 157	Followed	2020	Pennsylvania	Trial	State
State Cases	Commonwealth v. Davis, 2020 PA Super 255	Followed	2020	Pennsylvania	Trial	State
State Cases	State v. Conner, 467 P.3d 246	Followed	2020	Arizona	Appellate	State
State Cases	State v. Gibbs, 2020 S.C. App. Unpub. LEXIS 301	Followed	2020	South Carolina	Appellate	State
State Cases	State v. Warner, 430 S.C. 76	Followed	2020	South Carolina	Appellate	State
State Cases	State v. Brown, 302 Neb. 53	Followed	2019	Nebraska	Supreme	State
State Cases	State v. Brown, 331 Conn. 258	Followed	2019	Connecticut	Supreme	State
State Cases	State v. Muhammad, 194 Wn.2d 577	Followed	2019	Washington	Supreme	State
State Cases	State v. Snowden, 2019-Ohio-3006	Followed	2019	Ohio	Appellate	State

Fig. 3: Document Variables

4   Developing a coding system

We used both a deductive and inductive process to develop our coding system. The research questions and our existing knowledge of the legal theories in Fourth Amendment issues enabled us to create a list of codes that we knew we would use. The full coding system was then developed through an inductive process in which we used paraphrasing. Each case was read and paraphrased (**Analysis > Paraphrase Document**) to explore three questions:

- ❖ What was the alleged crime in the case?
- ❖ What third-party doctrine tool did the case involve?
- ❖ What legal doctrines were utilized, and what arguments did the court make to justify their decision?

The paraphrases were then explored in the Categorize Paraphrases tool available in the **Analysis > Paraphrase** menu, and codes were developed from them. This was not a purely inductive process, as we had initial categories, but there were several groups of codes that were developed entirely through the paraphrasing.

4.1 Preparing for analysis—restructuring part of the coding system

When the documents were all coded, it became apparent that the coding system would benefit from restructuring. The original coding frame had complex hierarchies with numerous sub-codes in our two primary categories, "Alleged Crime" and "TPD utilization" (Tools used by police without a warrant). To be able to effectively analyze the data, reducing the number of sub-codes made sense, not only for comparative analysis but to eliminate codes that were only assigned to 1 or 2 cases. Both "Alleged Crime" and "TPD utilization" were ultimately reorganized into new top-level codes "Crime groups" and "TPD groups."

For example, in the original coding of "Alleged Crimes," there were 8 sub-codes for different types of property crimes, but most of them were used only a few times. We initially had coded cases with both the generic "Property crime" code and the specific sub-code. We decided that it made more sense to have a more streamlined coding system and thus created the new top-level codes under the heading "Crime groups." We duplicated each of the individual sub-codes in the original "Property Crime" heading and then merged all the duplicates. We right-clicked on the code and selected **Duplicate Code with Segments**, which created a new code (for example, in addition to "arson", there was now a code "arson (1)" in the code system). We then selected all of the duplicate codes in the category and merged them, renaming the code "Property." This code was then moved to the new top-level code "Crime groups."

This gave us a simpler coding system (Fig. 4) which became important when analyzing the data. Were we to do this again, we would have begun with a simpler set of alleged crimes, and just used comments on coded segments to identify the specific type of crime.

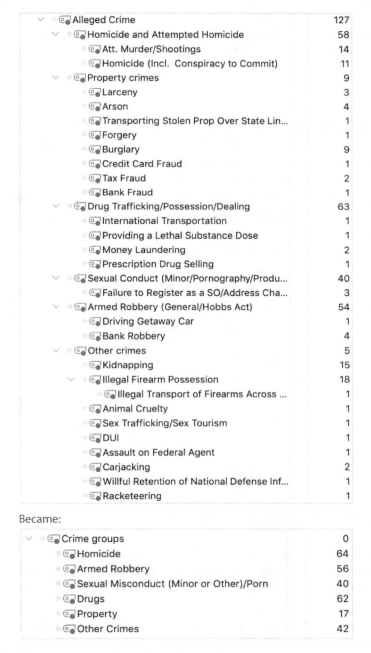

⌄ Alleged Crime	127
⌄ Homicide and Attempted Homicide	58
Att. Murder/Shootings	14
Homicide (Incl. Conspiracy to Commit)	11
⌄ Property crimes	9
Larceny	3
Arson	4
Transporting Stolen Prop Over State Lin...	1
Forgery	1
Burglary	9
Credit Card Fraud	1
Tax Fraud	2
Bank Fraud	1
⌄ Drug Trafficking/Possession/Dealing	63
International Transportation	1
Providing a Lethal Substance Dose	1
Money Laundering	2
Prescription Drug Selling	1
⌄ Sexual Conduct (Minor/Pornography/Produ...	40
Failure to Register as a SO/Address Cha...	3
⌄ Armed Robbery (General/Hobbs Act)	54
Driving Getaway Car	1
Bank Robbery	4
⌄ Other crimes	5
Kidnapping	15
⌄ Illegal Firearm Possession	18
Illegal Transport of Firearms Across ...	1
Animal Cruelty	1
Sex Trafficking/Sex Tourism	1
DUI	1
Assault on Federal Agent	1
Carjacking	2
Willful Retention of National Defense Inf...	1
Racketeering	1

Became:

⌄ Crime groups	0
Homicide	64
Armed Robbery	56
Sexual Misconduct (Minor or Other)/Porn	40
Drugs	62
Property	17
Other Crimes	42

Fig. 4: Reorganizing the coding system into more concise groups

5   Analyzing coded data

Once the documents were coded, we began the analysis by exploring the data in order to begin to look for patterns and themes in the data and to identify the frequencies of specific codes. This process was repeated for each of our research questions. For this chapter, we will provide an example of how we analyzed the data beginning with types of crime and third-party doctrine surveillance and evidence-gathering tools.

5.1 Code Frequencies

We started exploring data by examining how often specific codes have been applied to our data. The function Code Frequencies made this a simple task. We activated the codes we wanted to examine, in this instance, the sub-codes of "Crime groups" and then selected **Analysis > Code Frequencies.** This generated a table that showed us the number of documents which contained each code together with the percentage breakdown (Fig. 5). Since a case could be coded with more than one criminal charge, the frequency totals are larger than the number of documents. Code Frequencies also permits you to view "Segments with code" but that was not needed for the nature of our data.

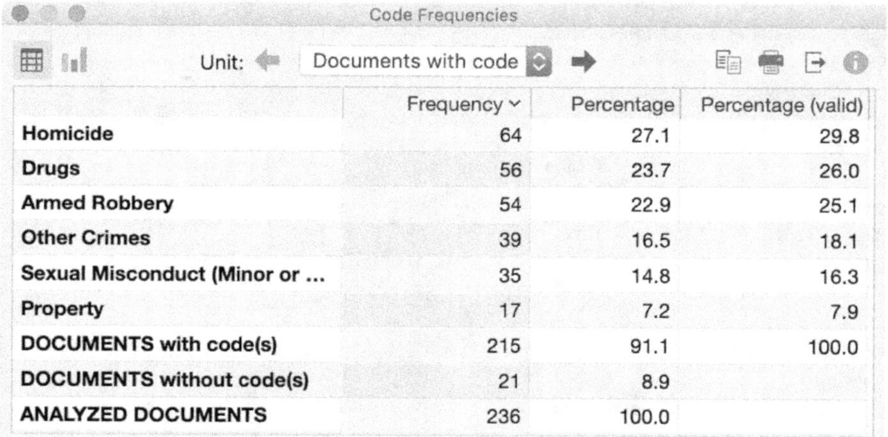

	Frequency ∨	Percentage	Percentage (valid)
Homicide	64	27.1	29.8
Drugs	56	23.7	26.0
Armed Robbery	54	22.9	25.1
Other Crimes	39	16.5	18.1
Sexual Misconduct (Minor or ...	35	14.8	16.3
Property	17	7.2	7.9
DOCUMENTS with code(s)	215	91.1	100.0
DOCUMENTS without code(s)	21	8.9	
ANALYZED DOCUMENTS	236	100.0	

Fig. 5:   Code Frequencies showing the number of documents containing a "Crime" sub-code

The second to the last row of the Code Frequencies table revealed that there were 21 documents without codes. Considering that every case involved a crime, this meant that there were documents that had not been coded for "alleged crimes." Since the original coding scheme included both codes for "alleged crimes" and then the specific crime as sub-codes, we right-clicked on the top-level code "Alleged Crime" and selected **Transform into Categorical Variable** to easily identify the documents without alleged crimes coded. To accomplish that, we activated documents by document variable selecting documents with an "<empty>" variable value in the new variable (**Mixed Methods > Activate by Document Variable**). We then reviewed each document and coded the missing crime type. The reviewing process also resulted in discarding five cases from the project that were not actual criminal cases.

Once the documents were all properly coded, we ran the Code Frequencies again to double-check our results. Next, we used the **Copy to clipboard** icon to make a copy of the table, and then created a code memo for the main category code ("Crime groups"). We pasted the frequency table into the memo, providing us with easy access to frequency data (Fig. 6). This process was repeated each time we used Code Frequencies.

The chart view of the Code Frequencies was also used (Fig. 7), and the chart was copied and exported as a graphic file to be possibly used in the final paper and presentation.

This entire process was repeated for two additional groups of codes, "TPD groups" and "Legal Doctrines." Once completed, we had a clear picture of the breakdown of cases in our data. For example, drug cases represented slightly more than a quarter (27%) of our cases, followed by armed robbery (24%) and sexual conduct with minors/child pornography cases (17%). The third-party doctrine tools codes were equally instructive, with almost half of all cases involving cell site location information (CSLI) (47%), and 34% of cases involving either efforts to obtain IP addresses or subscriber info for specific internet accounts.

Crime groups	Frequency	Percentage	Percentage (valid)
Homicide	64	27.71	27.71
Drugs	62	26.84	26.84
Armed Robbery	56	24.24	24.24
Other Crimes	42	18.18	18.18
Sexual Misconduct (Minor or Other)/Porn	40	17.32	17.32
Property	17	7.36	7.36
DOCUMENTS with code(s)	231	100.00	100.00
DOCUMENTS without code(s)	0	0.00	-
ANALYZED DOCUMENTS	231	100.00	-

Fig. 6: The use of code memos to provide descriptive statistics about the top-level group

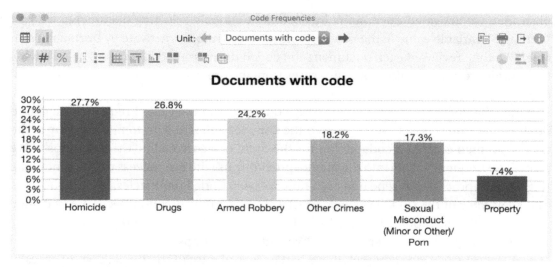

Fig. 7:   Chart view of Code Frequencies for use in final paper

5.2 Co-occurrence of codes: Code Relations Browser

The next step in our analysis was to compare how third-party doctrine (TPD) tools were distributed by crime types. The Code Relations Browser (available in the **Visual Tools** menu) is the ideal tool for this task. We activated the codes in the "TPD Groups," and navigated to the Code Relations Browser. Here there are several options (Fig. 8). We chose **Activated codes for rows**, **Choose top-level code** for columns, and **Occurrence of codes in same document** for type of analysis.

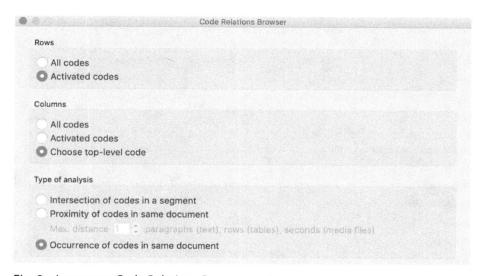

Fig. 8:   Important Code Relations Browser options

When prompted for the column top-level codes, we chose "Crime groups" and this resulted in a Code Relations Browser as shown in Fig. 9. The default view presented the relationships of codes with different sized squares. We then used the Heat Map option to focus on the key differences in the data.

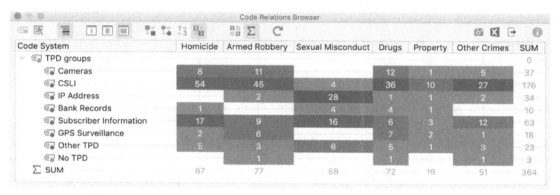

Fig. 9: Code Relations Browser used to demonstrate the relationship between crime type and third-party doctrine (TPD) surveillance tools

The Code Relations Browser helped us see the clear difference in the use of TPD tools by crime types. For example, surveillance cameras were used in every category except sexual misconduct with a minor/child pornography cases but was most prevalent in armed robbery and drug cases. Internet IP addresses and subscriber information was used across many crime types but was most common in the sexual conduct cases. If our sample was a random sample (instead of a complete population of cases), we could have used MAXQDA Stats to confirm the hypotheses that differences were statistically significant by calculating crosstabs and p values for example. With this information in hand, we were ready to begin to explore the data more carefully.

5.3 Retrieved Segments

We were not surprised by the prevalence of IP addresses/subscriber information in the sexual miscconduct cases, as it makes sense that cases involving child pornography would include requests for internet data. But we wanted to dig deeper into the data. We began by double-clicking the cell for IP Address/Sexual Misconduct and then shifted to the Retrieved Segments window.

In this window, all 57 text parts from 28 documents coded with both codes were compiled (Fig. 10). This provided us with access to all of the documents with these two codes. While we could scroll through them, MAXQDA provides better tools to do a deeper analysis of the data. We used three of the options in the title bar of the Retrieved Segments window: the Smart Coding Tool, the Overview of Coded Segments, and Word Cloud.

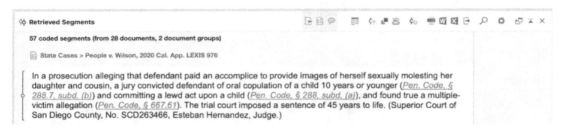

Fig. 10: Compiling relevant coded segments in the Retrieved Segments window

The Overview of Coded Segments and the Smart Coding Tool accomplish much of the same in terms of scrolling through the coded segments, but we chose to utilize the Smart Coding Tool, because it provides the ability to view the segments in tabular view, with access to any code comments, and shows all of the codes linked to each segment (Fig. 11). It is a true multi-purpose tool that can be retrieved from several places within MAXQDA. The comments column is editable, and you can add additional comments as you are examining the data.

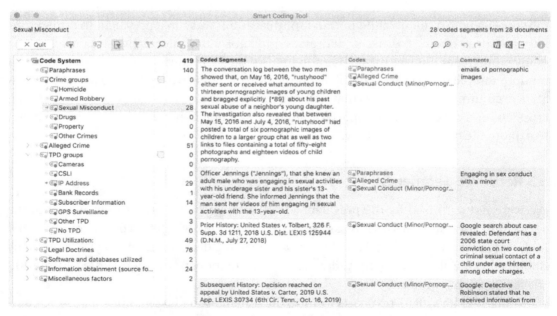

Fig. 11: Using the Smart Coding Tool to examine coded segments and add comments

The Smart Coding Tool enabled us to gain deeper insights into the data, at a micro-level, looking only at one specific set of coded segments. We turned next to the Word Cloud feature within retrieved segments, not because we wanted to create a visual representation of our data (although we could certainly do that later in the process of writing) but because we wanted to investigate the context of specific words that appeared in the Word Cloud. Accessing Word Cloud from Retrieved Segments, instead of from the main menu item (**Visual Tools > Word Cloud**), has the advantage of only using the words that appeared in the Retrieved Segments window. It is a valuable way to get a picture of the prevalence of what was included in that particular sample (Fig. 12).

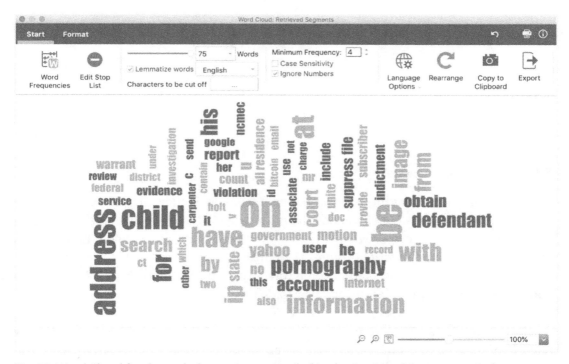

Fig. 12: Word Cloud for the coded segments compiled in the Retrieved Segments window

The Word Cloud's true power of analysis is the ability to view its underlying data. While viewing the Word Cloud, we double-clicked on a term, for example, "address" and this produced the results of a search for the term "address" within the retrieved segments. We were able to read through how the word appeared in the data and began to identify patterns and underlying context (Fig. 13).

Like with the Smart Coding Tool, the Word Cloud search results could easily be copied, further coded, and exported. Together these tools provided us with a richer understanding the reasons why IP addresses were found in combination with sexual misconduct cases.

Preview	Beginning	Document group	Document n...	End	Search item
number(s) used to access the Internet, email addresses, connection address, current/recent IP addresses, and any identifying in	27	Federal Cases	United State...	27	address
the Internet, email addresses, connection address, current/recent IP addresses, and any identifying information, which would te	27	Federal Cases	United State...	27	addresses
analyzed at length the Carpenter decision and its applicability to IP address information. See United States v. Kidd, 394 F. Su	144	Federal Cases	United State...	144	address
two intersecting sets of cases." Id. at 360. "The first set of cases addresses a person's expectation of privacy in his physica	144	Federal Cases	United State...	144	addresses
this Court previously deemed a potentially "apt comparison for IP address information," the Supreme Court "found that recording	145	Federal Cases	United State...	145	address
were violated on June 26, 2006, when his I[nternet] P[rotocol] address was seized [*3] without warrant or judicial approval" i	22	Federal Cases	Christie v. Bl...	22	address
"storm," a user is expected to make his Internet Protocol (IP) address available to all the other members of his group by stayi	21	Federal Cases	United State...	21	address
billing records, records of session times and durations, and IP addresses and cookies [*2] linked to the accounts used by Defe	20	Federal Cases	United State...	20	addresses
is a type of virtual currency. Each Bitcoin user has at least one "address," similar to a bank account number, that is a long s	55	Federal Cases	United State...	55	address

Fig. 13: Use of Word Cloud to further examine common words in coded segments

5.4 Code Matrix Browser

We next wanted to look at the same cases while seeing how they differed by our two primary groupings of cases. While the documents are divided into two Document Groups of state and federal court cases, we also have created document sets based on how the case was characterized by *Shepard's Citations*. Did the case directly follow the precedent from *Carpenter* or was it distinguished in some way? The Code Matrix Browser (**Visual Tools > Code Matrix Browser**) provided an easy way to do this.

We began by going back to the Code Relations Browser and double-clicking on the cell for IP Address/Sexual Misconduct. This activates all of those documents and codes. We navigated to the Code Matrix Browser, selected document sets to be displayed in the columns and chose to restrict the display to only activated documents and codes and limited it by using the option **Count hits only once per document**. It produced a table that provided a simple breakdown (Fig. 14). The matrix shows us that 21of the cases came from distinguished cases, and 6 were listed as following the precedent.

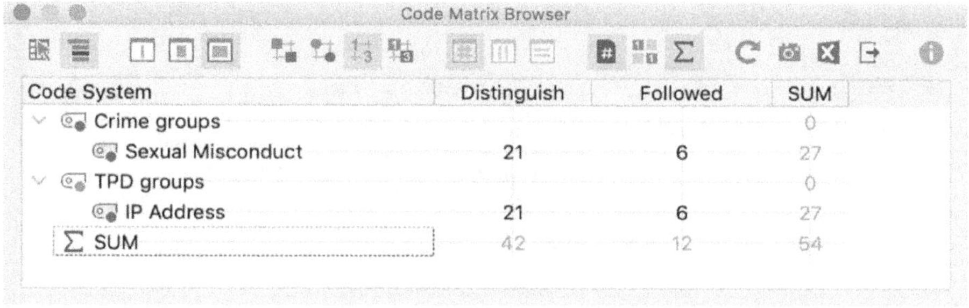

Code System	Distinguish	Followed	SUM
∨ 🔲 Crime groups			0
🔲 Sexual Misconduct	21	6	27
∨ 🔲 TPD groups			0
🔲 IP Address	21	6	27
Σ SUM	42	12	54

Fig. 14: Code Matrix Browser view analysis by document sets (in the columns)

With this information, we could double-click on either cell (21 or 6) and view the retrieved segments for those cases, and further examine them using the tools described above (Retrieved Segments, Smart Coding Tool, and Word Cloud).

5.5 Summarizing coded data in the Summary Grid

At this point, we were ready to conduct the final stage of analysis for this particular combination of codes. We wanted to go further in our analysis of the sexual conduct cases to gain a deeper understanding of how these cases were similar and different. There are many ways to accomplish this. We could go to the Smart Coding Tool and add new codes to provide greater depth in the analysis, but we chose to use MAXQDA's Summary Grid tool to create a Summary Table that would be an essential part of our final research product.

Writing summaries in the Summary Grid (**Analysis > Summary Grid**) can be thought of as similar to paraphrasing, in that it lets the user take a segment of a document and summarize it in your own words. The difference is that the Summary Grid is used to summarize already coded data. And once summarized, that information can be compiled in a table, exported into a table document, exported out of MAXQDA, or even used to create a concept map in MAXMaps.

To create the summaries, we activated the Sexual Misconduct and IP Address codes to be able to limit the Summary Grid to the relevant codes. We then right-clicked on the Sexual Misconduct code and selected **Activate Documents Containing this Code**. This enabled us to limit the Summary Grid to the relevant cases. We then navigated to Summary Grid, in which each cell with a blue dot indicates that there is at least one coded segment with the specific code (row) in the document (column). We read each one and wrote a brief summary of main points (Fig. 15). Once summarized, the cell turned green, and when all of the blue dots were "green" we were done with the task.

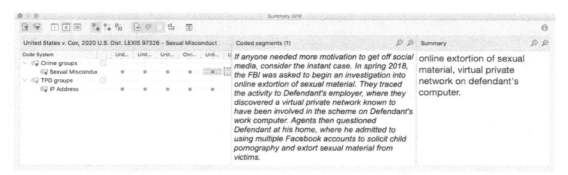

Fig. 15: The Summary Grid is used to create concise summaries of coded segments

Once completed we opened the Summary Tables view (**Analysis > Summary Tables**) and created a new table, including the codes "Sexual Misconduct" and "IP Address." We also selected several document variables, including "Year," "Shepards," and "Case Name."

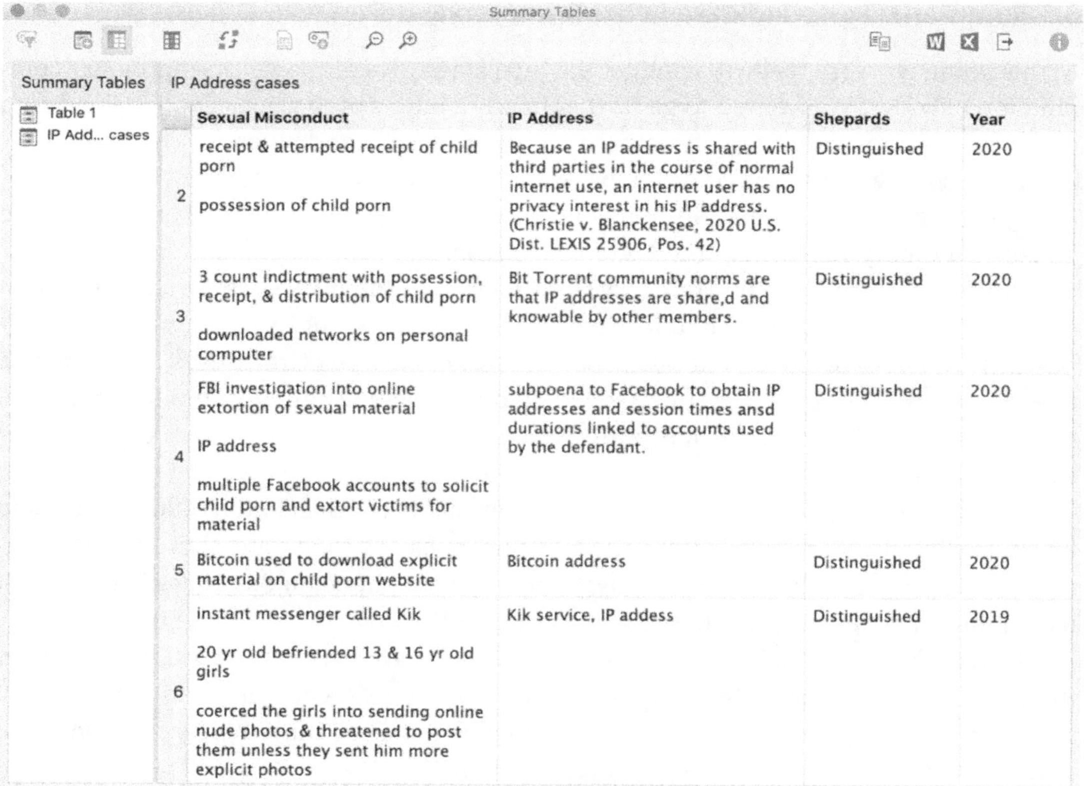

	Sexual Misconduct	IP Address	Shepards	Year
2	receipt & attempted receipt of child porn possession of child porn	Because an IP address is shared with third parties in the course of normal internet use, an internet user has no privacy interest in his IP address. (Christie v. Blanckensee, 2020 U.S. Dist. LEXIS 25906, Pos. 42)	Distinguished	2020
3	3 count indictment with possession, receipt, & distribution of child porn downloaded networks on personal computer	Bit Torrent community norms are that IP addresses are share,d and knowable by other members.	Distinguished	2020
4	FBI investigation into online extortion of sexual material IP address multiple Facebook accounts to solicit child porn and extort victims for material	subpoena to Facebook to obtain IP addresses and session times ansd durations linked to accounts used by the defendant.	Distinguished	2020
5	Bitcoin used to download explicit material on child porn website	Bitcoin address	Distinguished	2020
6	instant messenger called Kik 20 yr old befriended 13 & 16 yr old girls coerced the girls into sending online nude photos & threatened to post them unless they sent him more explicit photos	Kik service, IP addess	Distinguished	2019

Fig. 16: A Summary Table of the cases involving sexual misconduct and IP address searches

The resulting table provided a concise summary of the cases that included the "Sexual Misconduct" code (Fig. 16). The Summary Table can be exported out of MAXQDA, but it can also be turned into a table document, where it could be further coded if necessary. For our project, the Summary Table was primarily used in writing the final results of the study. We included several Summary Tables in the final paper.

6   Lessons learned

This chapter has provided a case study of one way of using MAXQDA to conduct a research project. It has demonstrated how the power of MAXQDA can be harnessed by undergraduates with little experience with the software. We believe that by following a similar process, students can achieve results using MAXQDA at a level significantly beyond what is reasonable for a traditional student research paper. With proper guidance, students can accomplish a lot with MAXQDA.

One lesson we learned from this process is to realize that every project is different, and the workflow we use will differ depending on the research questions being answered and the nature of the data. It is important to recognize that you do not need to know every tool MAXQDA offers. We selected an analytical process that made sense for our questions. There were other ways we could have proceeded, and other tools we did not even consider. Just because MAXQDA offers a smorgasbord of qualitative research tools does not mean you have to eat everything that is on the table. We chose a set of tools that made sense given our questions, and which could be easily used for each of the questions we examined. It makes sense to have one systematic process in mind, which you can adjust to an individual project by selecting the appropriate tools for each main step. Typically, these are literature reviews, data exploration, coding data, analyzing coding data, and transforming insights into a final report or paper.

To determine what that looks like for a project will take some exploration, and obviously the more familiar you are with the software and its options, the easier it is to establish a workflow. While the "guide map" of steps we chose made sense for this project, an entirely different approach might be selected with a different research question. For example, in this project, we knew that many of the cases being studied would have a result unfavorable to the defendant, because the factual circumstances of the cases occurred before *Carpenter v. United States* was decided. Knowing this, our research questions were generally not focused on "who won" but instead on exploring how courts were evaluating third-party doctrine issues. This caused us to select a specific set of analytical tools. If our goal was to see how *Carpenter* impacted the outcome of cases, we would have centered our coding scheme on that issue and quantified our results to do more of a mixed methods approach, with both the qualitative descriptions of what happened in cases and also used statistical analysis to look for correlations and do comparisons of how case outcomes and legal reasoning differed in state and federal courts.

Finally, it's important to know that this process occurred over the course of a semester. The undergraduate students had no prior experience with MAXQDA and were able to learn how to use the software to conduct the literature review, and use the analytical tools described above, with just a few tutorial overview sessions. MAXQDA is a powerful software tool, with numerous analytical techniques, but it can be successfully used with just a few hours training. Indeed, much of the process described in this chapter was first included in a brief handout with step-by-step instructions and screenshots of how to do it. And then we walked through each task together. We found that stepwise learning is a highly effective approach in teaching MAXQDA in a research class. We did not teach all of the tools that are in MAXQDA, but only those necessary to accomplish the next step. This process of learning avoided having the user overwhelmed by all of the features in MAXQDA. Thus, in the beginning, we taught data management and writing memos, then paraphrasing and literature reviews. In the next step, we turned to coding and finally analysis, with a particular focus on visual tools.

Bibliography

Canon, B. C. & Johnson, C. A. (1988). *Judicial policies: Implementation and impact* (2nd ed). CQ Press.
United States v. Jones, 565 U.S. 400 (2012).
United States v. Miller, 425 U.S. 435 (1976).
Smith v. Maryland, 442 U.S. 735 (1979).
Carpenter v. United States, 585 U.S. ___ (2018).

About the authors

Michael C. Gizzi is a professor of criminal justice at Illinois State University, USA. He has a PhD in political science from The University at Albany, SUNY. He has used MAXQDA since 2014 in various legal research projects and teaches MAXQDA in research courses, workshops, and webinars.
ORCID: https://orcid.org/0000-0002-9130-7969
ResearchGate: https://www.researchgate.net/profile/Michael-Gizzi

Alena Harm is a master's student in criminal justice at Illinois State University, USA, graduating in 2021. She has a bachelor's degree in criminal justice and psychology and has used MAXQDA in graduate work for two years.

Using MAXQDA for Analyzing Focus Groups: An Example from Healthcare Research

Matthew H. Loxton

Abstract

This chapter will discuss the ways in which MAXQDA supported the collection, analysis, and reporting of our focus group data related to healthcare improvement. It deals mainly with one specific study regarding the activation of a new primary care facility (PCC), but also draws from many other examples where focus groups were used. The chapter describes our use of MAXQDA focus group features, Word Clouds, and Keyword in Context, as well as use of Visual Tools such as the Document Portrait, Code Relations Browser, and Code Matrix Browser. The chapter also deals with importing variables, and use of memos, paraphrases, and summaries related to focus groups. The use of Lexical Search, code imports, and auto-coding are also covered.

Key MAXQDA features covered	
✓ Import Focus Group Transcripts	✓ Word Cloud
✓ Lexical Search	✓ Keyword-in-context
✓ Autocoding Search Hits	✓ Paraphrasing
✓ Speaker Variables	✓ Summary Grid
✓ Document Portrait	

1 Introduction

Hospitals are multi-domain expert communities in which collaboration, science, and evidence are prioritized, but frequently silos of expertise or specialty-focus result in processes that are fragile, poorly meet patient needs, or are mutually corrosive. High-functioning processes in one department often result in chaos for another. We have found focus groups to be very useful in bridging silos, identifying key issues, and exploring new methods.

Popularized by Merton at the US Bureau of Applied Social Research at Columbia University in 1946 (Lee, 2010), and possibly first described as a method by Bogardus in the 1920's (Jackson, 1998), focus groups have been used extensively in varied applications, such as marketing, public relations, political campaigns, product design, quality management, and computer user experience and interface design. Focus group studies have enjoyed broad adoption as a relatively low-cost and moderately effective means to explore open-ended questions with small groups of people selected to represent some target population, to test ideas, products, concepts, or scenarios, elicit reactions and sentiments, and spark innovation.

Our focus group sessions often included the use of discussion prompts such as product examples, images, audio tracks, or video clips. Some involved walking through a location, such as a ward floor, surgery, or other medical environments. These artifacts and events required capture and analysis within MAXQDA.

We used the full array of MAXQDA's rich functionality for analysis and reporting on focus group data, including metadata variables, analysis and mixed methods tools, visual tools, and reporting. We also used MAXQDA statistical analysis and comparison tools. Going back to the initial description by Bogardus of a "group interview" (Bogardus, 1926), we used two kinds of group interviews: traditional and nominal focus groups.

1.1 The traditional focus group

The traditional focus group presumes a group setting in which members have direct interaction with each other and participate in a generative process in which one participant's input might build upon another's. This assumption of strong interaction and role of the agents as participants, rather than subjects, is a key feature of the traditional focus group. As a result, each participants' text needs to be coded both as an individual, and in context of their interaction with others.

A risk with traditional focus groups is that some participants may unduly influence others, and the presence of observers, bosses, or outsiders as participants may inhibit the free flow or expressions of opinions, experiences, or ideas of others (Van Bennekom, 2002). For the traditional focus group, we therefore coded interaction types that existed between the participants, and between participants and the moderator.

1.2 The nominal focus group

Borrowing from the concept of the *nominal group technique* (Gallagher, Hares, Spencer, & Bradshaw, 2017), the nominal focus group solves the risk of undue influence from other participants or observers by having no formal group at all.

We frequently used this approach, and selected individuals who had a shared *weltanschauung*, traditions, or occupational environments implying a latent exchange of beliefs, opinions, and assumptions. Members of these nominal focus groups were not ever in the same session or in a group interview setting, but there was a reasonable supposition that they were in direct or indirect communication as part of their shared characteristics. Putting all the transcripts together in a single document allowed us to use the focus groups Transcripts import functions and treat them as if they had been in a common session.

For example, we individually interviewed several nurses from different wards in the same hospital and formed a nominal group. While they were never in the same session, the degree to which they shared occupational experiences and commonality of work, allowed us to combine their transcripts into a single nominal focus group document. We grouped their responses by question, as if they had been in the same session, and had responded to each question in turn.

From a data perspective, the nominal focus group implies a need to capture the selection process and argument as part of the project data.

1.3 Data and coding considerations

One general approach to focus group coding is to view the coding requirements in terms of analytical levels. Kuckartz and Rädiker (2019) propose the following four analytical levels:

❖ Topic
❖ Participant
❖ Group Interaction
❖ Moderator

In our focus groups, we typically coded to suit a set of phenomenologically grounded topics—typically related to what the participants felt "worked well", had negative outcomes, or where they believed there was a missed opportunity. In specific, our coding typically focused on topics related to healthcare delivery; policy implementation, medical or allied technology deployments, or changes to clinical or administrative workflow.

Our coding typically related to participants such as healthcare stakeholders, including researchers, clinicians, administrators, and patients. Participants increasingly included patients, patient advocates, and caregivers. Our focus group coding accommodated group interactions, especially in the sense of participant-participant interactions, but also situations in which the moderator interacted with participants or acted as a participant.

From the descriptions of the traditional and nominal focus groups above, several data types were identified in our studies.

1. Transcripts of sessions
2. Audio and video recordings of the sessions
3. General session notes captured by the moderator(s)
4. Participant interaction notes captured by a moderator
5. Audio, image, or video artifacts used as prompts
6. Planning and logistical notes

7. Data related to characteristics of the participants, such as age, gender, role, position, salary, race, accreditations, etc.

In some cases, we used multimethod and mixed methods approaches with focus groups to explore or explain shifts, spikes, or dips in operational metrics, as well as why policy, technology, or workflow adoption had been different to expectations or between groups. More recently, with the trend towards performing *appreciative inquiry* studies, we are using focus groups to assist in providing the "thick" account of what is working well, and potentially lead to innovation by exploring the contexts and dynamics of positive outliers in the measurements.

For example, we used an existing patient safety code system in conjunction with combined phenomenological, ethnographic, and grounded theory approaches to unpick root causes and uncover unexpected dynamics and forces of change. These approaches were augmented in some cases by running natural language processing (NLP) tools on the participant contributions in order to quantify sentiment. The quantitative metrics, root causes, and sentiment analysis enabled us to weave a powerful reporting narrative, and may have helped to effect changes in policy, technology, and workflow.

Although these focus group studies varied considerably in size, duration, make-up, and topic focus, some elements were frequently used across all projects, including:

❖ Existing code corpus for quality and safety. The code system included dimensions and facets that cover safety, timeliness, effectiveness, efficiency, equitability, patient-centeredness, and accessibility of care delivery and supporting services.
❖ Quantitative data from a wide variety of healthcare sources, that included incident statistics and details, patient flow measurements, patient outcomes metrics, and operational throughput and performance data. These included Control Charts from statistical tools such as R, Minitab, or SAS.
❖ Sentiment analysis data from tools such as R.

2   Preparing and importing focus group data

MAXQDA provides wide flexibility in data import and capture. For focus group data, specifically, MAXQDA allows the researcher to import transcripts with or without timestamps, but more crucially, allows speaker changes to be easily specified in the text. If the **Focus Groups Transcripts** function encounters a ":" symbol in the first 63 characters of a paragraph, it assumes the preceding sentence text is the name of a speaker, and the subsequent text is what they said. Fig. 1 shows an edited transcript without timestamps in a Word document that has been prepared for import.

Interviewer 1: Hi. So just some background. Like I said before, we are working with various primary care stakeholders to help set up and facilitate planning and workflow development sessions for activating the Ambulatory Care Center (ACC) in October. XXXXX suggested that you would all be able to help us to get some detailed insights on the patient and staff flow aspects of current day to day operations.

Interviewer 1: Can we start with introductions? Can you describe your role and involvement in the project?

Participant 1: I am in PCMH, only one of a a few now. Am one of the unit managers team leader for unit 1. One unit is offsite, and I am unsure how their workflow is done. Right now each unit is under a nurse manager, and I have been working in a nursing home for 2-3 years, as well as the OR, doing med-surg. Last 4 years I was in primary care.

Unit 1 has three care managers and we are short staffed. Have 8-9 doctors but they are part time. Two medical residents. Only clinic operating on Saturday, but that is the NP.

Participant 2: Hi

Interviewer 1: Hi What is your role, and how long have you been here?

Participant 2: Hi, I've been at XXXXXXXXX for 12 yrs. I currently coordinate the mental health program and intake using the biopsychosocial model. I also cover crisis care management. I was recently taken on as acting supervisory psychology role, but I wasn't previously directly involved in the care integration team

Participant 3: Sorry. Can you repeat that first bit again? Is this to do with the flow workshop?

Interviewer 1: Sure! Hi, yes we are working with XXXXXXXXXX to help set up and facilitate the workshop next week for planning and workflow development for the new facility, especially the integration of primary care and mental health in the new facility. XXXXXXXX suggested that you would be a good person to provide us with some insights on the patient and staff flow aspects of current day to day operation.

Fig. 1:   Edited transcript

When imported, MAXQDA creates a code with the name of the speaker, and auto-codes the text with that code. Fig. 2 shows the results of importing the same transcript, and the count of coded segments (participant contributions) is reflected in a number to the right of the code.

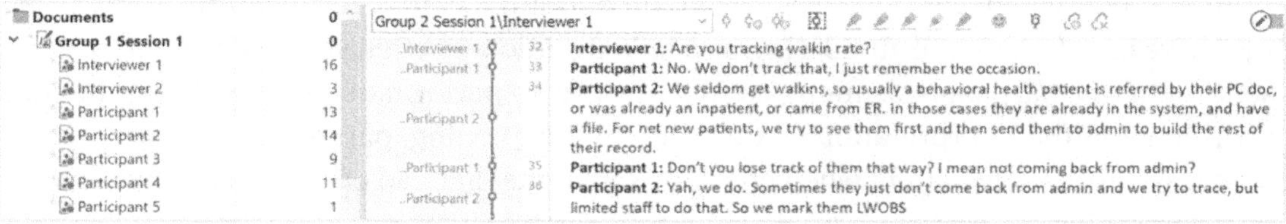

Fig. 2:   Imported focus group transcript in MAXQDA's Document System (left) and Document Browser (right)

Note: Each speaker should start with a new paragraph, and the speaker name, i.e., the characters to the left of the colon, should be no more than 63 characters (including spaces). To avoid inappropriate associations in the text, it is therefore necessary to remove all colons that are not associated with speaker changes prior to importing. In this example, the transcript file was pre-edited to have speaker names and topics in boldface simply to aid readability, but was not required by MAXQDA for coding.

After importing focus group data, we found it prudent to begin by reviewing the Document System and Code System window to ensure all files were imported, all participants and moderators were represented, and no unexpected participants were listed. Unexpected items in the Document System or Code System were typically the result of errant colons in the first 63 characters of a line in the transcription text, or variation in the spelling of participant names. The easiest corrective action was to make a note of all the unexpected items, and then before doing any other work in MAXQDA, use the **Undo (Ctrl/cmd+Z)** function to back out of the import, and correct the issues in the source transcription text.

MAXQDA will sort the codes in both the Document System and Code System window in the order in which the text was encountered in the transcript. The order in the display can be changed in both Document System and Code System by right-clicking on the parent code and using the **Sort function** to sort alphabetically or by frequency, or by simply dragging the code to the desired location in the hierarchy. Any changes in the order made in the Code System will automatically be reflected in the Document System pane. As with any other document type, focus group documents can be added to document sets. Adding a focus group transcript to a set can be accomplished by dragging and dropping the document onto a preexisting set. Additionally, if a number of focus group documents are activated prior to creating a new document set, they will automatically be added to the new set when it is created.

Where recorded sessions were allowed by our client and agreed to by participants, we used Skype to record the sessions. We auto-transcribed the audio files using an online transcription service. We found this to be highly cost-effective, and it reduced our workload. Although the audio files are large, we typically imported these and linked them to the transcripts so that whenever there was any doubt about the context or meaning of a text segment, we had the original audio. Having a linked audio was often very useful to identify the sentiment of a particular segment, as well as a way to perform quality checks on the transcription and the interpretation by our team in their coding, paraphrases, or summaries. This was particularly helpful when checking segments that had critical meaning, or to verify if something contradictory was said with sarcasm or in irony.

> Note: If transcripts contain timestamps, these will be removed by MAXQDA once the associated media file has been assigned to it. If no transcript is available, the full features of the inbuilt MAXQDA transcription tools are available.

3   Navigating the focus group data and auto-coding

Once satisfied that all and only the expected participants have a code in the Document System and the Code System, it was useful to review each of the transcripts to establish that they were intact and complete. By double-clicking on the document name (in the example in Fig. 2, "Group 1 Session 1"), the full transcript is listed in the Document Browser pane. Double-clicking a participant code displays the Coded Segments pane listing, and a preview of all the coded segments representing what that participant said (Fig. 3). Clicking on any of the rows in the Coded Segments pane results in a preview of the segment text, as well as highlighting the associated text in the Document Browser.

Fig. 3:   Participant coded segments (contributions)

Right-clicking the document name in the Document System results in the context menu which now has an additional entry, **Focus Group Speakers**. Clicking on "Focus Group Speakers" results in an overview pane (Fig. 4). The content of the pane can be filtered by clicking on the **Only activated focus group speaker's** icon.

The table provided us with an overview of the number of coded segments and coverage associated with each participant. It was an early indicator of whether one or more participants were outliers, and either dominated the discourse or were mostly silent. We exported the numerical values and graphs for use in our progress reports. The table view also gave us the ability to add new user variables. In this example, the variable "Role" has been added to distinguish between the major work divisions at the hospital. Variables can also be accessed by going to the "Variables" section in the ribbon bar, and clicking the **List of Speaker Variables**, or the **Data Editor for Speaker Variables** icons.

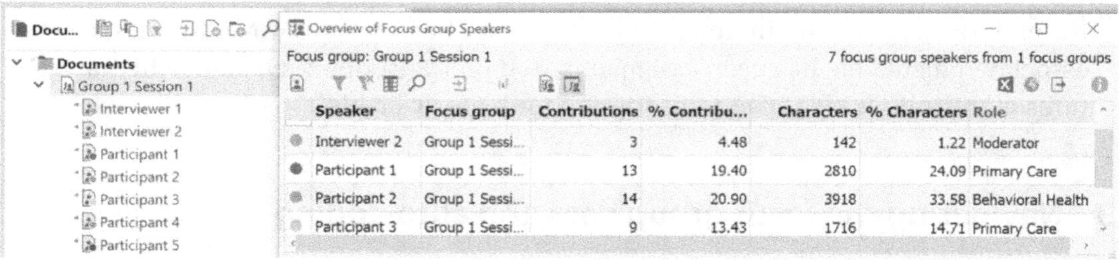

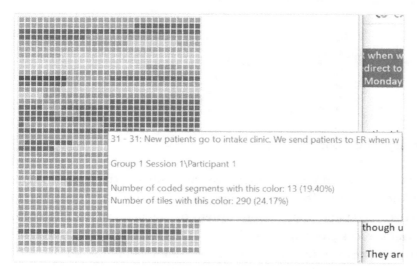

Speaker	Focus group	Contributions	% Contribu...	Characters	% Characters	Role
Interviewer 2	Group 1 Sessi...	3	4.48	142	1.22	Moderator
Participant 1	Group 1 Sessi...	13	19.40	2810	24.09	Primary Care
Participant 2	Group 1 Sessi...	14	20.90	3918	33.58	Behavioral Health
Participant 3	Group 1 Sessi...	9	13.43	1716	14.71	Primary Care

Fig. 4: Overview of Focus Group Speakers

We assigned participant codes different colors to gain a similar perspective on contributions by using the **Document portrait** function in the context menu (Fig. 5). In that case, grouping the participant codes by color quickly revealed if any participant groups or individuals tended to be outliers in their number or distribution of contributions. This was particularly useful in detecting if the moderators tended to over-talk, but also helped to see if some participants spoke more or less frequently than others, or at different times than others. Hovering the mouse over any specific tile reveals a short preview of the text and some basic descriptive statistics that were often useful just to orientate the researcher.

Fig. 5: Document Portrait

The portrait view in this example shows some expected results, such as that the moderators (light blue) started the dialogue, are scattered throughout, and are not overly represented. However, it also alerted us to the fact that the sessions did not terminate with the moderator—no light blue at the end. This is an example of not seeing an expected element in the visualization, and which prompted us to query if text was cut off prematurely.

Clicking on the **Ordered by color frequency icon** yielded a further revelation—purple (Participant 5) contributed almost nothing (Fig. 6). Clicking on the purple tiles takes the Document Browser view to the associated coded segment, and in this example, revealed that Participant 5 quit the session shortly after it started, and was lost to contact. These tools gave us a quick, but highly effective overview of the data, and highlighted potential issues upfront.

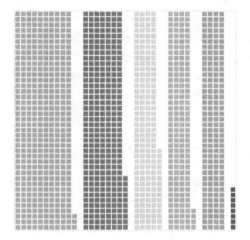

Fig. 6:   Document Portrait—ordered by participant

We used **Visual Tools > Word Cloud** as a further data orientation feature, which in conjunction with a stop list and activating only the participant codes, gave a tabular, and also a graphic view of the most frequent words in the transcript. We used **MAXDictio > Word Frequencies** and **MAXDictio > Word Combinations** to see frequencies of multi-word phrases.

From a methodological point of view, we see this as an important step in gaining a broad overview of the "voice of the corpus" prior to reading the transcripts. The argument is that frequency of words and phrases is a good initial indication of what was most salient to the participants, and perhaps an early insight into elements of the coding that will likely be required. We also used it to compare word or phrase clouds of different strata of participants. For example, we could see if the participants from one facility, or one role, or one gender used different terms to another grouping, or used terms more or less frequently than another. This was useful, for example, in identifying potential power gradients between different groups by the language that predominated in the Word Cloud and frequency table.

The Keyword-in-context (KWIC) function (available in the **MAXDictio** menu) retrieves text preceding or trailing a specified keyword. This function allowed us to look for keywords in the context of surrounding text and therefore notice patterns and nuances that may otherwise have escaped attention.

Fig. 7 shows instances of occurrence of either "handoff" or "hand-off" across all participants. For this focus group, the KWIC raised three points for further exploration—firstly, it was unexpected that participants would refer to both "warm" and "hot" handoff of patients. "Hot-handoff" was an expected result of recent changes and a defined facility term, but there was no such thing as a "warm" handoff in the project lexicon. Noticing the use of "warm-handoff" as a term helped identify that clinicians were not always able to achieve the desired handoff, but counted as "warm" those that "almost satisfied" the requirements. Secondly, since the handoff was a critical success factor for integrating Mental Health and Primary Care at this facility, eight occurrences was unexpectedly low. Thirdly, the clinician who used the qualifier "when it happens" raised further questions as to what was causing handoff failure. This is an example of how our research often followed the path of the data, rather than stick to the letter of the session topics.

Keyword-in-context					— □ ✕
Keywords: handoff; hand-off				8 hits in 2 documents and 0 document groups	
Document	**Be...**	**Context**	**Keyword**	**Context**	
Group 1 Session 1	48	our ability to get hot-	handoff	to MH. We used to	
Group 1 Session 1	50	that. Participant 4: The hot-	handoff	, when it happens, works really	
Group 2 Session 1	57	I now often get hot-	handoff	from PC, and it homes	
Group 2 Session 1	59	really pleased with the hot	handoff	. I would like to see	
Group 2 Session 1	60	...tered. Participant 10: Concur. Hot	handoff	allows us to move vulnerable	
Group 2 Session 1	67	the team and do warm	handoff	for voluntary or involuntary admission	
Group 2 Session 1	33	messages. Patients need a warm	hand-off	rather than hunting down through	
Group 2 Session 1	58	the idea of the hot	hand-off	between PC and MH, but	

Fig. 7: KWIC function

4   Creating and importing Speaker Variables

Similar to how document and code variables are handled in MAXQDA for other data types, the Variables tab in the ribbon menu has a function to provide a **List of Speaker Variables**, as well as a **Data Editor for Speaker Variables**. As the names imply, the former is a quick way to list all existing user-defined variables or create new variables. The latter function reveals the values of the variables associated with each speaker. The **Import Speaker Variable** function can save time compared to manually entering them in MAXQDA. We used this feature to import desired speaker variables such as gender, ethnicity, employment level, job title, etc. from a human resources database. To do this, we first created a single user-defined variable in MAXQDA, exported as a Microsoft Excel sheet to get the exact structure required, and then merged the external data into the Excel sheet, and imported into

MAXQDA. Fig. 8 shows the List of Variables pane superimposed on the Data Editor after variables were imported for Facility and Gender.

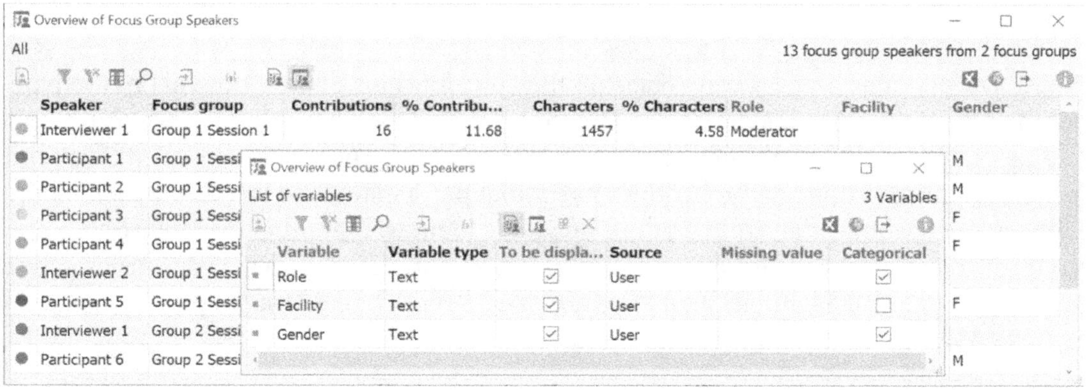

Fig. 8:   Focus group Speaker Variables

In addition to being able to import speaker variables, MAXQDA allowed us to **Export Speaker Variables** (available as an icon to the right in the Overview of Focus Group Speakers or in the **Variables** tab), for use in external software or as part of a report. The **Variables > Speaker Variable Statistics** function shows tabular or graphic frequencies or percentages.

4.1 Focus group data coding

Once we had oriented ourselves by looking through the transcript, viewing the document portrait, and examining word, phrase, and KWIC results, the more fine-grained task of coding and analysis began. We approached focus group transcripts much like any other interview or document, and used memos, summaries, and paraphrases to annotate, interpret, or demarcate the speaker contributions as we read through the transcripts. What may be different in addressing focus group data is the need to note interactions *between* participants.

We adopted three basic approaches in reading the focus group transcripts. For the Primary Care Center focus groups that we studied, we used just the first of the following methods, but in other projects, we have used a combination, or all the methods in conjunction.

1. Read the full transcripts in order of occurrence. This gives an overall perspective of the sequence, and may help to identify any maturing or shift in how topics were presented, or how the moderators may have adapted over time.
2. Read the combined transcripts for each topic. In many projects, the same topics or questions are posed to several groups over a period of time. Reading by topic, gives a strong narrative perspective of the group responses to the topic.

3. Read the transcripts by participant. This approach gives a perspective of the contributions of a single participant at a time and allows the researcher to gain closer understanding of themes, habits, or styles of each participant that may otherwise have been lost in the interaction.

MAXQDA provides an easy way to see all the contributions of an individual participant. Right-clicking on any specific participant code in the Document System, will result in a context menu with the **Overview of Contributions** option. The resulting Coded Segments pane provides a listing of all contributions for that participant, and has all the familiar options to select some or all contributions and code them with another existing code, a new code, or to export the list in several formats. Fig. 9 shows an example of this process, and the resulting Coded Segments pane. The **Analysis > Smart Coding Tool** function is also available for focus group coded segments.

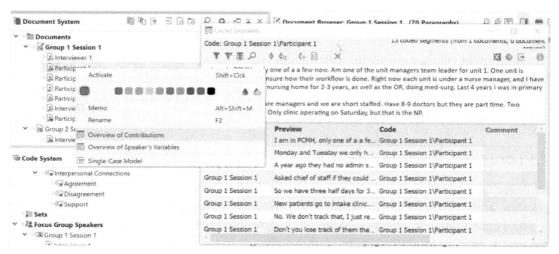

Fig. 9: Overview of Contributions

Memos

As with other types of research, memos are often added prior to coding, and used as a vehicle to develop codes. For our focus group coding, we made extensive use of in-document memos and found it an excellent way to store specific moderator or observer notes related to a segment. This often included any notes about reactions that one participant had to the speech or actions of another, or moderator behavior that may have influenced participants. For example, in one session, a nurse clapped her hands to her face when another spoke of a near-miss due to confusion between two similar-sounding but very different medications. This would be very difficult to capture in a transcript, but if it appears in moderator notes, it can be attached to the relevant segment as an in-document memo.

Likewise, in-document memos were used to record events such as the details of a prompt, or a walkthrough. Memos were also used to record moderator notes to themselves, such as *"Participant-2 rolled her eyes when the topic of the ePortal was raised, and I am unsure what this meant. We did not get another chance to ask her to elaborate."* Notes of this kind were helpful to remind us during the coding phase of events that changed the meaning or implications of the transcription text, or that needed to be followed up.

The in-document memos were also frequently used as a record of possible code suggestions by different team members. Memos that contained follow-up suggestions or questions were given the "?" memo label [?]. This feature was used extensively in a nominal focus group project related to patient experience of radiology, and were a crucial means to communicate between the researchers.

Paraphrases

Paraphrases accurately, but concisely state the meaning of a particular text. This was important in our focus group settings when one or more participants interrupted or interjected when another was speaking. In these cases, it was sometimes necessary to piece together a participant's full contribution in order to present it in its full and uninterrupted form. It was a challenge because a contribution sometimes spread across several paragraphs and interleaved with other speakers. An effective approach was to construct the precis and attach it to the participant's initial text where they first started a train of thought as a paraphrase.

This re-ordering could not be done in the transcript itself without destroying the sequence and interaction, so it was done as a paraphrase.

The paraphrase tools (**Analysis > Paraphrase**) include options to categorize existing paraphrases, view a paraphrase matrix, or print the current document including paraphrases. We used the Categorize Paraphrases function to assist in developing new codes. This function was especially useful in developing new codes, because it provided a side-by-side view of original vs paraphrased text.

Pre-designed code systems

We typically used elements of existing code systems specifically designed for focus group analysis, or which are institutional or traditional to the healthcare industry. For example, the group interaction coding system developed by Morgan and Hoffman (2018), is specifically designed for focus groups and to address the interaction between participants. In Fig. 10, there is an example of the Morgan and Hoffman coding system, that has been slightly adapted for our use in MAXQDA. This was imported using the **Import Codes and Memos from Excel Spreadsheet** function in the **Codes** menu.

Fig. 10: Morgan and Hoffman group interaction coding system

In retrospect, what may improve the Morgan and Hoffman coding structure, is a way to indicate the directionality of interaction, and researchers may wish to apply codes to indicate directionality of group interaction that is specific to their study topic. For example, it may be important to note whether it is a male interrupting or supporting a female, or whether doctors support nurses.

There are many possible approaches to coding this directionality, but here are three that you may consider (points 2 and 3 courtesy of Stefan Rädiker):

1. Create a family of "directionality" codes specific to the context. For example, if I want to depict male vs female directionality, I might have the following codes "M->F", "F->M", "F->F", and "M->M", and then code any segment reflecting a directional action or speech act. Used in conjunction with the Morgan & Hoffman Group Interaction system, the directionality codes applied to the same segment could denote, for example, that a male disagreed with a female.

2. Another approach using codes and variables, is to create a code family for "Target of Action" and duplicate all the participants and moderators as sub-codes. In this case in a speech act by "Participant-1", we might code the segment as being "Support", and code it with the "Target of Action" as "Participant-2" to show who did the supporting, and who received the support. The participant variables could contain biographical data such as gender, and therefore allow us to show by gender, who was supporting whom by using the **Visual Tools > Code Relations Browser**.

3. A third option is to use the **Edit comment** function (e.g., by right-clicking on a coding stripe in the Document Browser) to add a text to the interaction code saying who ad-

dressed whom. This function can be accessed in the context menu for a coded segment. For example, by clicking on the coding stripe in the Document Browser.

Some code systems are typical to an industry. For example, in healthcare, it is common to have a number of codes specifically related to safety that will always be applied to any interview or focus group transcript in addition to any codes developed for that specific study or derived through a grounded theory approach. Such "institutional code systems" may be applied more easily through the use of standardized search terms such as described in the next section.

Bulk coding

We used the Lexical Search tool (**Analysis > Lexical Search**) to search within the transcripts, and to bulk-code segments in focus group transcripts matching pre-determined codes. This feature saved time when applying codes that related to searchable constructs. For example, searching clinician transcripts for "patient safety" OR "hazard" OR "hospital acquired", etc. made it easier to identify and code segments relating to patient safety prior to a complete read-through of the transcripts. To save time and reduce inter-coder variance, complex search strings were saved and reused. In general, the researcher can apply any institutional coding relatively quickly, and thus not detract too much from the core focus of a specific focus group project, although care must be taken not to let bulk coding obscure the need for careful analysis and coding.

5   Focus group analysis

For us, coding and analysis overlapped and were often iterative, since development of our Summaries typically involved analysis, and informed further coding. During analysis, there were typically adjustments or further development of codes, and it was rare that codes remained unaltered during the analysis phase of our projects.

5.1 Summaries

Paraphrases religiously reflect the voice of the participant, but the summary reflects the voice of the narrator. We used summaries to provide the significant events, exchanges, and meanings of a transcription segment in our own words, as well as our analysis of meaning and implication. As such, there was overlap between how in-document memos and summaries were used to code focus group transcripts.

In-document memos were typically created *before* coding and as a means to develop codes, whereas the summaries were developed *after* initial coding was done. A summary reflected all the segments for a specific existing code within a document, and was therefore typically created *after* initial coding. Summaries provided an analysis for reporting, but were also used to develop additional codes or make code refinements. We frequently used summaries in our progress reports, and it gave us a good overview of the focus group coding as a whole. To a large degree, the summary content was directly transportable to the final report and reflected the process and results of analysis. MAXQDA provides a toolbox for developing summaries and shows all coded segments for a topic per focus group as a Summary Grid.

Fig. 11 shows a Summary Grid in which a code that denotes questions between participants related to the transcript for "Group 1." The center column contains the original transcript text of the coded segments, with a highlighted hyperlink to the Document Browser location. The right column contains the researcher's description of the text. In the first segment we are summarizing the transcript context as part of the patient registration process in an ambulatory clinic. The second text summary in the example refers to staff access to the electronic health record (EHR) system.

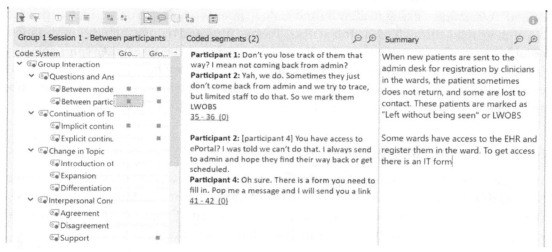

Fig. 11: Summary Grid

The summaries were typically the skeleton of what went into our reports, and together with text quotations, and ideas in in-document memos and comments on coded segments, formed the basis of our analysis. In practical terms, once summaries had been completed, there was often little left to do other than piece together the narrative of a report from the confluence of these four sources. Where necessary, we would support a point or assertion by providing instances of quoted transcript text or images derived from the Crosstabs, Code Relations Browser, or MAXDictio Word Clouds. We found it especially useful to build Word Clouds in MAXDictio by setting the word combination to 2–5 words and applying lemmatization and a stop list. This helped us to demonstrate frequently used phrases, such as "warm handoff," which was highly salient terminology for our client. In one project, we were able to show that there was broad staff acceptance and support for the "Hot-Handoff" concept, but that there were issues that reduced its effect. We could show that the changes in policy had not led to any increases in reportable incidents and accidents, by drawing from statistical analysis of facility safety reporting data, and coupling that with qualitative analysis that gave an understanding of why staff were satisfied with the new processes. We were also able to identify gaps in processes and reporting that should be addressed in a follow-up initiative.

MAXQDA provides two other tools related to summaries: The Summary Table offers a compilation of summaries, and we found this useful for presentations and reports, while the Summary Explorer enabled us to compare the summaries of different cases or groups.

6 Lessons learned

MAXQDA has proven to be an effective tool for analysis and reporting of focus group data in our healthcare setting. The following are a few lessons learned:

❖ **Clean before you import.** Don't assume data from a transcription service, or a video clip or audio track, are clean. They may require significant editing and cleaning prior to import and may require highly specialized tools that take time to acquire. Plan ahead and conduct dry runs and tests before running a live session. For example, in a video clip of a focus group on "patient flow" there was detail in the background that showed patient information. It needed someone with special graphic tools to blur the background in the clip before importing.

❖ **Determine beforehand how prompts will be captured.** In some focus groups, prompts are used to initiate discussion, and may be the object of the discussion. For example, a set of images might be shown to the participants, and then several questions related to the image will be posed. The prompt might be patient record to examine, a video clip to watch, or a software app, a tool, or an in-situ walkthrough of a process. These prompts need to be represented in some fashion in the data, which may take significant forethought and planning.

❖ **Be prepared for dealing with conflicts between the participants.** It is not to say a conflict resolution expert will be needed, but it is wise to prepare responses in case conflicts arise between participants.

❖ **Consider how you will deal with "narrator's voice" and significant actions.** For example, when a participant got a call and left, we added that as text in square brackets in the transcript. In retrospect, this was a mistake, because it then counted as their contribution. Before the session, think through how you will denote, code, and use events like people entering or leaving, dropping things, etc. Will you code them as "actions" perhaps, and add a **Code Comment**, or will you add a memo, or do something else?

❖ **Plan how large media files will be handled.** Audio and video files for an entire 90-minute focus group session can become very big. Plan ahead for where you will store these files, and how archiving and backups will be managed. We kept media files on a thumb-drive, but this very quickly filled up, and made access to the files from within MAXQDA slow. Moving them to a large-capacity USB-3 hard-drive improved things.

❖ **Consider using more than one recording device.** We experienced a hardware failure and lost the recording of an entire session. Once media files are uploaded, ensure all backups are complete before deleting any data from the recording device.

Bibliography

Bogardus, E. S. (1926). The group interview. *Journal of Applied Sociology, 10*(4), 372–382.

Gallagher, M., Hares, T., Spencer, J., & Bradshaw, C. (2017, 1). The nominal group technique: A research tool for general practice? *Family Practice, 10*(1), 76–81. https://doi.org/10.1093/fampra/10.1.76

Jackson, P. (1998). Focus group interviews as a methodology. *Nurse Researcher, 6*(1), 72–84. https://doi.org/10.7748/nr.6.1.72.s7

Kuckartz, U., & Rädiker, S. (2019). Analyzing focus group data. In *Analyzing qualitative data with MAXQDA: Text, audio, video* (pp. 201–217). Springer Nature Switzerland. https://doi.org/10.1007/978-3-030-15671-8_15

Lee, R. M. (2010). The secret life of focus groups: Robert Merton and the diffusion of a research method. *The American Sociologist, 41*(2), 115–141. https://doi.org/10.1007/s12108-010-9090-1

Morgan, D. L., & Hoffman, K. (2018). A system for coding the interaction in focus groups and dyadic interviews. *The Qualitative Report, 23*(3), 519–531. https://nsuworks.nova.edu/tqr/vol23/iss3/2

Van Bennekom, F. C. (2002). *Customer surveying: A guidebook for service managers.* Customer Service Press.

About the author

Matthew Loxton is a Principal Analyst at Whitney, Bradley, and Brown Inc. focused on healthcare improvement and strategic foresight, serves on the board of directors of the Blue Faery Liver Cancer Association, and holds a master's degree in knowledge management from the University of Canberra.
ORCID: https://orcid.org/0000-0003-3650-596X
ResearchGate: https://www.researchgate.net/profile/Matthew_Loxton

Using MAXQDA for Analyzing Documents: An Example of Prioritization Research Design in Urban Development

Temur Gugushvili, Gvantsa Salukvadze

Abstract

Prioritization research design is an approach to identify priorities in development strategies on various areas using MAXQDA. The design incorporates a combination of different methodological approaches, including systematic literature review, evaluative qualitative text analysis, and transformative mixed methods research. This chapter provides an example of an urban development issue in the city of Gori, Georgia. We highlight the usage of four MAXQDA tools, the Smart Coding Tool, Complex Code Configurations, Document Portrait, and MAXMaps. The Smart Coding Tool was used to re-check the codes and coded segments for consistency in coding according to the methodology and to create and apply evaluative codes in addition to thematic codes. Complex Code Configurations was used to illustrate the distribution and frequencies of the combination of thematic and evaluative codes. MAXQDA's visual tools (MAXMaps and Document Portrait) enabled us to present the links between the urban development dimensions and evaluative codes. The Document Portrait was used to depict the proportion of text segments dedicated to each urban development issue in the analyzed documents. MAXQDA made it possible to synthesize and quantify document variables and thematic and evaluative codes. Ultimately, it enabled us to examine urban development issues in a way that brought together globally-promoted principles, while considering local peculiarities.

Key MAXQDA features covered

- ✓ Import Document Variables
- ✓ Coding
- ✓ Memos
- ✓ Smart Coding Tool
- ✓ Code Configurations
- ✓ MAXMaps
- ✓ Document Portrait

1   Introduction

The 21st Century era has raised unique challenges for urban settlements and the development of many cities around the world still hinges on outdated urban planning approaches. Urban planning is often hindered by low planning trends, which serve as barriers to development and divorce global goals from accurate localization. Even though many international policy documents[1] outlined guidelines for inclusive and sustainable development, the real obstacle of how to execute global or national objects on the local level remains. Every settlement is a dynamic organism, shaped by centuries of events that create distinctive characteristics and form vibrant destination-specific identities. These historical details make the transformation of global principles into local solutions even more difficult.

This study is part of the urban planning project related to the completion of a "Basic Plan" for the city of Gori, which will serve as a strong foundation for the city's forthcoming "Master Plan" for land usage. The project was implemented by the City Institute Georgia (CIG), a non-profit organization focused on sustainable urban development. Gori is located in eastern Georgia and serves as a connecting highway between the country's western and eastern regions, and was a focal point in the five-day Russian-Georgian war in 2008, causing displacement of the local population. As a result, war has bought fundamental changes and new challenges for the future development of Gori. A particularly important issue on the city's urban development plan was to integrate large-scale new settlements, which were constructed both in the city and in its surrounding area after the resettlement of internally displaced persons during the war.

After a thorough analysis of possible methodological approaches to achieve the stated aim of developing a land use master plan for Gori, we realized there was no one approach that could solve the problem of matching globally promoted urban principles with the needs of a specific locality or region. To fill that gap, we devised an approach that we call "prioritization research design," which draws on the tools of qualitative and mixed methods data analysis including systematic literature review, evaluative qualitative text analysis, and transformative mixed methods. MAXQDA has provided a valuable platform to integrate all of these different forms of analysis to execute this new approach. The research design was developed in a way to handle information appearing from different sources (policy documents, articles, research reports, expert interviews, participatory workshops). As a result, the analyzed data integrates both, globally-promoted principles (e.g., international development strategies, agendas) and local characteristics of the case study area.

---

1   See, e.g., such as the Sustainable Development Goals (Goal 11 – Sustainable Cities and Communities), https://www.globalgoals.org/11-sustainable-cities-and-communities; New Urban Agenda (Habitat III), http://habitat3.org/the-new-urban-agenda/; and the EU/Georgia Association Agreement, https://eur-lex.europa.eu/legal-content/EN/TXT/PDF/?uri=OJ:L:2014:261:FULL&from=EN.

2 Data collection

The first phase of our research design utilizes principles of systematic literature review (Petticrew & Roberts, 2006). A comprehensive literature search was conducted based on the following inclusion criteria: latest international policy documents promoting sustainable urban development principles, local, regional strategic vision documents, primary research findings related to urban issues of targeted city Gori, etc. After collecting the relevant literature materials, the files were imported into MAXQDA and distributed in the predefined document groups created in the Document System. The documents were grouped according to the following thematic sub-groups, such as International Urban Development Agenda, Urban Development Agenda, National Policy, Regional Development/Strategic Vision, Research Findings. As a result, up to 10 documents were included into the five different thematic categories (Fig. 1).

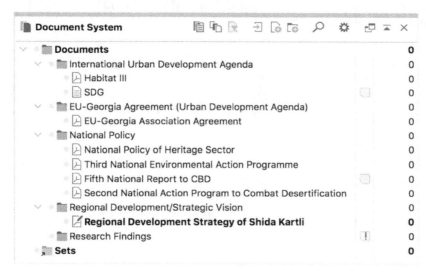

Fig. 1: Literature organized in the thematic folders

3 Including document variables as background information on the documents

It was necessary to collect additional variables that would provide essential background information about each document being studied. Four variables were added:

1. *type of document* differentiated three kinds of documents (urban development plan, policy, research findings). It was used to determine what type of documents were most prevalent and, conversely, what kind of documents were in short supply;

2. *document-level* grouped documents by international, European, and national levels. The information obtained from this indicator was finally considered when allocating priorities of the urban development priorities through counting points;

3. *subject* variable aggregates information about what issue the document served to address (e.g., general and specific, such as cultural, environmental). Accordingly, it was used to determine whether the paper focused on a particular issue(s) or was general. With the help of this, it became clear how diversified the selected, and existing documents were;

4. *publication date* provided us with information about the time of publication of the paper, which was important in terms of timing as the latest documents were required for the study.

It should be noted that in the first stage, the attribute information about documents was collected in Microsoft Excel format, and then imported into MAXQDA via **Variables > Import Document Variables** (Fig. 2 and 3).

	A	B	C	D	E	F
	Document group	Document name	type of document	document level	subject	publication date
1						
2	National Policy	National Policy of Heritage Sector	policy	national	cultural heritage	2014
3	Regional Development/Strategic Vision	Regional Development Strategy of Shida Kartli	policy	national	General	2013
4	EU-Georgia Agreement (Urban Development	EU-Georgia Association Agreement	urban development agenda	EU	General	2015
5	International Urban Development Agenda	Habitat III	urban development agenda	international	General	2016
6	National Policy	Third National Environmental Action Programme	policy	national	enviromental protection	2017
7	International Urban Development Agenda	SDG	urban development agenda	international	General	2015
8	National Policy	Fifth National Report to CBD	research findings	national	enviromental protection	2017
9	National Policy	Second National Action Program to Combat Deser	policy	national	enviromental protection	2014

Fig. 2: Attribute information in Excel file (before importing)

Data editor - All documents   8 Documents

Document group	Document name	type of document	document level	subject	publication date
International Urban ...	Habitat III	urban development agenda	international	General	2016
International Urban ...	SDG	urban development agenda	international	General	2015
EU-Georgia Agreem...	EU-Georgia Association Agreement	urban development agenda	EU	General	2015
National Policy	National Policy of Heritage Sector	policy	national	cultural heritage	2014
National Policy	Third National Environmental Action...	policy	national	enviromental protection	2017
National Policy	Fifth National Report to CBD	research findings	national	enviromental protection	2017
National Policy	Second National Action Program to ...	policy	national	envaromental protection	2014
Regional Developm...	Regional Development Strategy of ...	policy	national	General	2013

Fig. 3: Attribute information in MAXQDA file (after importing)

4   Building the coding frame for (evaluative) qualitative text analysis

The initial code system was developed integrating basic concepts of evaluative qualitative text analysis (Kuckartz, 2014). A hybrid approach was applied in which several text segments were assigned to the initially developed codes/sub-codes. First, pre-set thematic codes have been defined with other teammates of the urban development project group at CIG, including *Internally Displaced Persons (IDP) Settlements, Tourism, Urban-rural Interconnection, Public Transport,* etc. Besides, various additional "emergent" data-based thematic codes were created and defined according to the visions and strategies reflected in the sampled documents.

The code system, alongside thematic codes, consisted of evaluative categories such as the *Scale of Discussion, Significance of Multiple Effects,* and *Validation of Discussion* (Fig. 4):

Scale of Discussion

During the coding process, it was apparent that there was a wide range in the documents in terms of how acute the problems are in the settlement and which should be considered in the urban development process. Based on this, the evaluative code *Scale of Discussion* was created, which assessed the addressed area of the debate through the above-mentioned indicator. The sub-codes reflected the different scale levels:

❖ Gori level (settlement Gori, municipality)
❖ Region level (Shida Kartli)
❖ Urban Settlements level (Georgia)
❖ National level (Georgia)

A code memo containing this description was attached to each sub-code.

Significance of Multiple Effects

The code *Significance of Multiple Effects* was created to capture if one particular problem had an impact on causing other issues. If such a cause was mentioned in the document, this part of the text was coded according to the following three evaluative sub-codes:

❖ high
❖ medium
❖ low

Each sub-code had a description in the form of a code memo containing the following information: high – 3 problems and more; medium – 1 or 2; low – 0.

Validation of Discussion

Finally, a *Validation of Discussion* code was created to distinguish the quality of evidence on which the thematically coded passages relied because, in the documents, some provided arguments that were not clearly reasoned and therefore not evidence-based. The following evaluative sub-codes were developed:

❖ without proof/argumentation [no sources cited, no evidence]
❖ with weak proof/argumentation [descriptive statistics, international examples]
❖ with strong proof/argumentation [the author refers to research results, target-effect analysis]

The principle of assigning codes, as explained in the brackets, had been included in code memos (Fig. 4).

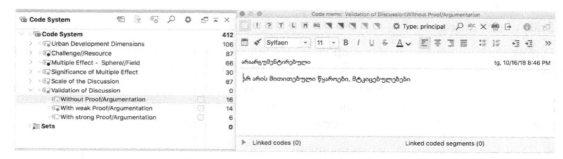

Fig. 4:   Memo of the evaluative sub-code "Without Proof/Argumentation"

5   Coding the data

As the documents were coded, it became apparent that additional codes needed to be added to the thematic codes, when the existing coding system didn't clearly capture all of the aspects of the themes. This ensured that all segments of the text could be coded. We chose the segment boundaries in such a way that the coded text segments were understandable outside their context, i.e., without the surrounding text. We ensured that code names very clearly reflected the content in the text. In the second stage, the created codes were revised, by shortening their names, writing them in a consistent style, and organizing them.

The revision process also included insuring that evaluative categories (*Scale of Discussion* and *Validation of Discussion*) were added to thematic ones. While many of these were done during the initial coding, it was not always possible, as some of the evaluative codes were developed in the middle of the coding process, and occasionally they were omitted by human error.

When working in a team, it is possible to divide coding responsibilities based on specific codes or on specific topics. We decided to divide the documents among the researchers to ensure that each document is read and evaluated as a whole, eliminating the possibility that only certain aspects are considered.

To check and to ensure that each thematically coded segment has been coded with the evaluative codes, too, we used the Smart Coding Tool (available in the **Analysis** menu). As shown in Fig. 5., the thematic code *Cultural Heritage* is selected in the left code tree and all its segments are listed in the right window. Here, the column "Codes" shows which additionally added evaluative codes have been assigned to each segment. The Smart Coding Tool was also used to apply the sub-codes of *Significance of Multiple Effects* to each thematically coded segment. Displaying all segments of one thematic category in the tabular form with all additionally assigned codes in an own column, immensely helped to assess the levels (high, medium, low) of the multiple effects of each urban development issue.

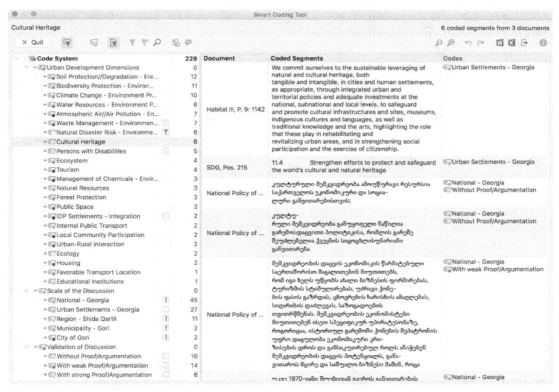

Fig. 5: Usage of Smart Coding Tool for assigning evaluative sub-codes to segments coded with thematic codes

6   Analyzing the coded segments

Coding the data prepared a baseline for the analysis of the coded segments. To assist in this process, we used several MAXQDA tools. These included Complex Code Configurations, MAXMaps, and Document Portrait.

6.1 Complex Code Configurations: Analyzing the co-occurrence of thematic and evaluative codes

Since prioritization research design puts great emphasis on both thematic codes and evaluative categories, Complex Code Configurations (**Analysis > Code Configurations**) were used to reveal percentages and frequencies of coded segments that were assigned both a sub-code of *Urban Development Dimensions* and a sub-code of *Scale of the Discussion* (Fig. 6). For example, in the highlighted row of the results table, we could see that the area of "National - Georgia" has been assigned to the same segment as "Atmospheric Air//Air Pollution - Environment Protection" twice.

Urban Development Dimensions	Scale of the Discussion	Segments	Percent
Atmospheric Air//Air Pollution - Environment Protection	Urban Settlements - Georgia	4	3.74
Atmospheric Air//Air Pollution - Environment Protection	National - Georgia	2	1.87
Atmospheric Air//Air Pollution - Environment Protection	Region - Shida Qartli	1	0.93
Biodiversity Protection - Environment Protection	National - Georgia	8	7.48
Biodiversity Protection - Environment Protection	Urban Settlements - Georgia	4	3.74
Climate Change - Environment Protection	National - Georgia	7	6.54
Climate Change - Environment Protection	Urban Settlements - Georgia	3	2.80
Cultural Heritage	National - Georgia	4	3.74
Cultural Heritage	Urban Settlements - Georgia	2	1.87
Ecology	National - Georgia	1	0.93
Ecology	Region - Shida Qartli	1	0.93

44 (of 115 theoretically possible) combinations

Fig. 6:   Complex Code Configurations for multidimensional analysis: Number of co-occurrences of thematic sub-codes (directions of urban development) with evaluative sub-codes (scale of discussion).

By checking the co-occurrence of the thematic code *Urban Development Dimensions* with the evaluative sub-codes of *Validation of Discussion*, the analysis revealed that substantial evidence is rarely presented when naming urban development issues. Insufficient information/evidence indicates, on the one hand, the need for additional research and, on the other hand, the fact that the provisions presented in the main strategies are not reliable.

6.2 MAXMaps: Creating concept maps showing the relations between the analyzed aspects

Data displayed in MAXMaps (**Visual Tools > MAXMaps**) proved to be the best way to portray information succinctly and efficiently, illustrating details provided in more comprehensive textual information. Fig. 7 shows a concept map illustrating the co-occurrences of the main thematic codes (in the center) with the three evaluative codes from our study (in the outer circle). The map was built based on the Code Co-occurrence Model (Code Intersection), which shows the code links by which same text segments were coded. The type of lines varies according to the codes and indicates family codes, whereas colors differ through different sub-codes.

The concept map added life to the coded qualitative data. It successfully depicted the research findings for analysis and presentation, and allows both researchers and readers to gain insights in a more effective way than just textual material. It clearly shows that tourism is mentioned in the context of the municipality, regional and urban development contexts without proof of argumentation, and it has a high impact on other urban development dominations.

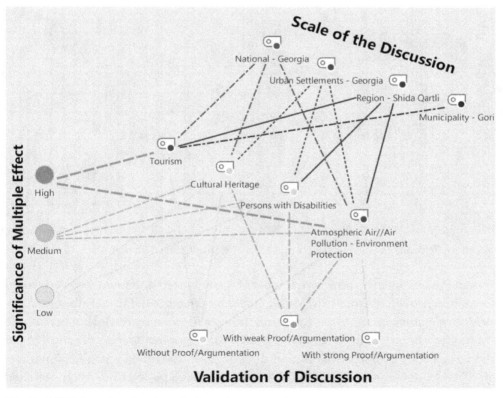

Fig. 7:   MAXMaps for visual analysis and presentation

6.3 Document Portrait: Visually comparing across documents and analyzing single documents

The utilization of the Document Portrait (**Visual Tools > Document Portrait**) has revealed several valuable insights of the analyzed documents, which were hidden throughout the whole analysis process. Each sub-code of *Urban Development Dimensions* was assigned different code colors, to be able to show the scale of discussion of each topic in MAXQDA's Document Portrait. Fig. 8 shows two Document Portraits with the option **Ordered by color frequency** switched on to illustrate which urban development issues are addressed in the analyzed documents. For the Shida Kartli Development Strategy document (A), tourism development, soil protection and degradation, IDP settlements (identified by the first three colors in the Document Portrait) are the most discussed topics. While a relatively big part of the text segments of the Urban Development Agenda/SDG (B) is also dedicated to the importance of tourism development in the urban context, followed by climate change and biodiversity protection (respectively the first three colors in the Document Portrait).

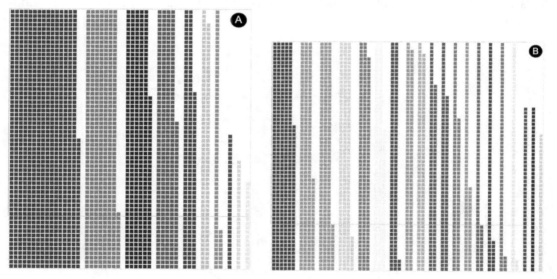

Fig. 8:   Document Portraits for cross-case comparison and single-case analysis

The Document Portrait clearly showed that most of the analyzed documents were devoted to the information provided about Gori Municipality (green color in Fig. 8) rather than the city of Gori (purple color in Fig. 8). At the same time, as for the city of Gori, it occupies a tiny part of the text/narrative in the text. Fig. 9 shows the proportional distribution of the scale of thematic codes (urban development directions) in the Shida Kartli Regional Development Strategy document. The MAXQDA option **Ordered by color** has been switched on for this purpose.

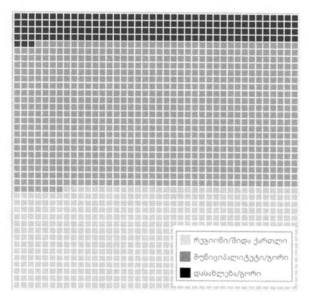

Fig. 9: Proportional distribution of the scale of discussion of thematic codes (directions of urban development) in the Shida Kartli Development Strategy document.
Yellow: region/Shida Karli; Green: municipality/Gori; Purple: city of Gori

6.4 Quantification of coded segments to rank priorities

Transformative mixed method research design (Driscoll, Salib, & Rupert, 2007; Tashakkori & Teddlie, 1998) has been employed to prioritize the urban development dimensions for the target city of Gori. Techniques for converting textual information, in particular, the quantification of qualitatively coded segments allowed us to use quantitative parameters for localization of global goals. The analysis included a description of qualitative and quantitative characteristics. Quantification was used to describe the quantitative parameters.

Each sub-code of the Urban Development Dimension was given a score according two crucial components:

❖ **Document-level** (international -> regional): The quantifying of the document level was carried out using the following principle: in the document group (e.g., international) one point is awarded in case of one code, and two points in case of two or more codes; this could be accomplished by using the Code Matrix Browser (**Visual Tools > Code Matrix Browser**).

❖ **The scale of discussion** (national -> settlement): According to the scale of the debate, points were awarded according to the following principle: *Georgia – 1 point; Urban settlement – 2 points; Shida Kartli – 3 points; Gori Municipality – 4 points; City of Gori – 5 points.*

As a result of the use of the prioritization research design, the areas of urban development were given appropriate weights to identify priority issues for the city of Gori in the urban planning process. Tab. 1 illustrates the calculated scores for each *Urban Development Dimension* using *Tourism* dimension as an example: Tourism was mentioned in all types of documents, particularly two times on international, European and regional level, whereas only one time on the national level. Therefore, in total, seven points were assigned to the tourism dimension for the document-level component.

Tab. 1: Calculation of points based on the document-level (example of dimension *Tourism*)

Document-level	Number of mentions in the document	Point
International	2	2
European	2	2
National	1	1
Regional	2	2
SUM		7

In the case of tourism, the scale of discussion was on the municipal level, which assigned four points to tourism issue. As a result, the sum of the seven points on the document-level and the four points from the scale of discussion amounted to a total of eleven points, which made tourism one of the top Urban development dimension for the city of Gori. The same principle of weight calculation was applied to other urban issues (see Tab. 2).

7 Lessons learned

This chapter highlighted how MAXQDA can be used for conducting a prioritization research design in urban development, focused on the Smart Coding Tool, Document Portrait, and Code Configurations. The smart coding tool proved particularly useful in dealing with the problem that coding rules that call for the assignment of multiple codes to one segment of text can often result in differences in coding among researchers and the need to refine the coding rules after initial coding. The Smart Coding Tool enabled us to easily review the segments we coded and adapt them to the updated rules/protocols. It can be used to revise, verify, and correct codes and code assignments simultaneously. More specifically, one of the coding protocols involved modifying a segment of the same text to determine whether it is encoded with different codes (e.g., thematic and evaluative). The Smart Coding Tool allows creating new codes by merging, splitting, or modifying existing codes. In our case, too, one of the evaluative categories was created entirely in the Smart Coding Tool.

Tab. 2: Prioritization of urban development dimensions

Urban Development Dimensions	Weight
Tourism	11
Climate change	11
Atmospheric air/air pollution	10
Biodiversity protection	10
Education	10
Soil protection/soil degradation	10
IDP settlement	9
Waste management	9
Water resources	9
Healthcare	9
Housing stock	8
Forest protection	8
People with disabilities	8
Cultural heritage	7
Community participation	7
Public transport	7
Urban Engineering	7
Natural Hazard Risk Management	6
Public and recreational spaces	6
Natural resources	5
Convenient transportation location	5
Cultural landscapes	4
Urban-rural connection	4
Chemical Substance Management	4

MAXQDA makes it easy to quantify the descriptive results of codes through Subcode Statistics. Code Configurations is an extremely valuable tool in going in greater depth to see not only the frequency of one code, but the frequencies of combinations of two or more codes. This made it much easier for us to evaluate the overall data we examined.

MAXQDA offers the researcher with a wide range of analysis and visual tools. These can be used to visualize data in ways that just reading documents can't. The Document Portrait was particularly helpful to see the ways that documents covered the thematic areas being studied. The grouping of the documents in combination with the assigned codes per document can be used to apply priority scores to which can be used as a basis to rank priorities.

Bibliography

Driscoll, D. L., Appiah-Yeboah, A., Salib, P., & Rupert, D. J. (2007). Merging qualitative and quantitative data in mixed methods research: How to and why not. *Ecological and Environmental Anthropology, 3*(1), 11. http://digitalcommons.unl.edu/icwdmeea/18

Kuckartz, U. (2014). *Qualitative text Analysis: A guide to methods, practice and using software*. Sage.

Petticrew, M., & Roberts, H. (2006). *Systematic reviews in the social sciences: A practical guide*. Blackwell. https://doi.org/10.1002/9780470754887

Tashakkori, A., & Teddlie, C. (1998). *Mixed methodology: Combining qualitative and quantitative approaches*. Sage.

About the authors

Temur Gugushvili is a PhD candidate in sociology at Ivane Javakhishvili Tbilisi State University. During his career, he has been mostly focused on the general policy orientation change from agriculture to rural development through different scientific and methodological stances. In this regard, for over six years, he has been handling various types of unstructured data with the help of MAXQDA.
Website: https://temurgugushvili.ge/ka/

Gvantsa Salukvadze is a PhD candidate in human geography at Ivane Javakhishvili Tbilisi State University. Since 2014 she has been using MAXQDA in various international scientific research projects, primarily to promote sustainable development in mountainous Georgia. From 2016 she also started teaching MAXQDA courses at different universities.
ResearchGate: https://www.researchgate.net/profile/Gvantsa_Salukvadze2

Using MAXQDA for Identifying Frames in Discourse Analysis: Coding and Evaluating Presidential Speeches and Media Samples

Betsy Leimbigler

Abstract

MAXQDA was used in my doctoral dissertation to uncover the types of frames used by American presidents and in media samples surrounding the contentious issue of health care reform at three critical junctures in U.S. history. The four main functions of MAXQDA used in this project included 1. creating and applying a sophisticated code system to hundreds of speeches and media samples, 2. using the Memo Editor and Overview of Memos to take notes, quickly summarize hundreds of documents, and highlight particularly outstanding or critical documents and patterns, 3. using the Code Frequencies chart functions, particularly using the unit of analysis "coded segments" to observe the number of codes used highlighting a certain major frame to then compare with other codes, and finally, 4. the Code Relations Browser function, which was particularly critical in highlighting the overlap, or co-occurrence of codes. This last function provided evidence for a major finding—that health care is not simply framed in one term (such as in economic terms), but rather in mixed ways (economic and human rights frames in particular). The co-occurrence function illustrates this pattern and confirms the presence of mixed frames. MAXQDA's tools provided a rich analysis into political and mediated discourse and supported the transformation of major public discourses on health care into frames through a deductive and inductive process.

Key MAXQDA features covered	
✓ Coding	✓ Code Frequencies
✓ Memos	✓ Code Relations Browser

1 Introduction

MAXQDA was used in my doctoral dissertation to uncover the types of frames used by presidents and in media samples surrounding the contentious issue of American health care reform at three critical time periods in U.S. history. Literature in political communication on issue framing has been growing rapidly as political science and political communication scholars seek to understand the power structures that shape policy and public opinion (Entman, 2004). Empirical studies conducted on media framing of policy issues confirm the importance of framing scholarship and the measurable existence of opposing viewpoints in public discourse (D'Angelo & Kuypers, 2010; Dorfman et al., 2013).

Frames can be identified in the discussions of politicians and media elites on health care reform. Qualitative and mixed-methods textual data analysis software is essential for conducting a frame analysis. Some of the most prominent frames in health care reform policy are "human rights vs. market commodities," raising the question of whether health care is a human right or a privilege; whether every person should have access to it, or whether it is primarily a good to be purchased. In addition, individualism, collectivism, and the state-federal government structure and financing relationship are further major ways in which health care is discussed in American public discourse. MAXQDA supported the transformation of these discourses into frames by providing the tools for a deductive and inductive process.

The project was guided by three main research questions:

1. How do frames emerge, evolve, and interact over time—both within and throughout each of the three critical junctures examined (1960s, 1990s, 2010s), based on the actor in question, and also within each critical juncture?
2. How do presidents and media frame health care reform proposals and attempts?
3. How are health care reform frames influenced by various institutional and historical contexts and public discourses, and consequently, what is the impact this has on trans-forming discourses into frames?

A qualitative study was most appropriate to assess the concepts that have been used around health care reform and to evaluate how reforms are influenced by various institutional and historical contexts.

2 Data collection and import in MAXQDA

Three critical time periods were chosen to investigate the relationship between elite discourse, media discourse, and the framing of a given federal health care policy or proposal. Large, landmark cases under democratic administrations were chosen, instead of only smaller, incremental reforms. The three critical junctures identified as the 1960s, 1990s, and 2010s are relevant given that these time periods in U.S. health care policymaking are widely viewed as significant, major windows of time focusing on federal health policy.

To explore the research questions concerning how frames around health care emerge and evolve, and how presidents and media frame health care reform, a substantial and systematic review of media samples and speeches was taken. Tab. 1 summarizes the dataset that was used. The American Presidency Project website was used to select 83 speeches over the three time periods.[1] In addition 257 media samples were selected through the Proquest (New York Times) database. Media sample selection occurred around the dates of each speech, with the 4 most relevant media samples found with +/–2 days of the given speech retained. The samples from the later time-periods were reduced for feasibility.

Tab. 1:   Collected speeches and articles

Time period	Speeches	Articles
1960s	11	32
1990s	21	71
2010s	51	154
Total	83	257

The MAXQDA project was structured around the research questions for the dissertation, namely: How do frames emerge and how do presidents and media outlets frame the issue of health care? Therefore, data was organized into six different document groups according to data set (three sets of presidential speeches, three sets of media samples, Fig. 1). All speech samples were in Microsoft Word format; media samples were in PDF format and were imported in the respective document groups.

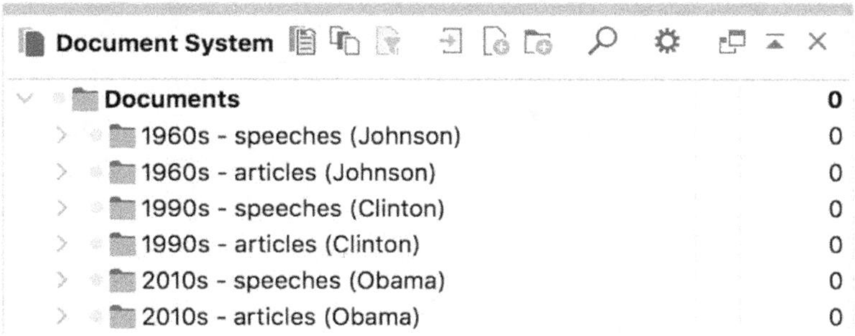

Fig. 1:   Data set grouped in document groups in MAXQDA's Document System

---

1   The relevance of speeches was evaluated manually. Speeches containing terms such as "health" or "Medicare", but concerning topics not directly related to health policy reform, were not included in the category of "relevance". One-sentence speeches and statements were also excluded. Also, The American Presidency Project database underwent design and filtering options changes during the time period of this research, and the new database may have different numbers for search terms than the ones outlined above, as the data collection occurred in October 2017.

The MAXQDA tools used for data exploration and analysis included 1) creating the coding frame with many sub-codes in the Code System window, 2) Memo Editor and Overview of Memos, 3) Code Frequencies for analyzing the usage of codes and sub-codes, and 4) using the Code Relations Browser to evaluate co-occurrences of codes.

3 Coding the data

A first step in this project involving MAXQDA consisted of coding and creating an entirely unique coding system related to health care and framing, as well as a code book to explain the application of the codes.

3.1 Setting up deductive codes and start first coding process

Six code categories were created, based on previous research on health care and framing. After importing the datasets into MAXQDA, the first coding process entailed assigning codes to segments of text that referred to each of these concepts, which were also defined using the code memos in order to increase precision and reduce subjectivity. The coding process started by using the six major discourses on health care as parent codes for the first coding process (Fig. 2). In other words, the six major discourses (Rights, Market, Individualism, Collectivity, Federalism, and States) were applied deductively to texts.

Code System	0
Rights	0
Economy/Market	0
Individual	0
Group	0
State	0
Federal	0

Fig. 2: Six deductive categories in MAXQDA's Code System window

One systematic way of uncovering health care reform frames is through a coding process that is both deductive and inductive—both having predetermined categories (deductive) as well as categories arising from the data (inductive) (Kuckartz, 2014). Thus, the code book was a key element of tracking how frames are used throughout each of the three critical junctures examined (1960s, 1990s, 2010s), based on the actor in question, and also within each critical juncture.

3.2 Creating inductive sub-codes in the first coding process

The inductive coding entailed additional codes or extra concepts being created and added to the code system while reading through the hundreds of speeches and media samples, including codes referring to who was being impacted, codes about education programs, about children, etc. By the end of the first coding process, which took several weeks, the code system had expanded from 6 to 92 codes.

New codes were added in the process of reading the speeches and media samples. As various topics around health care reform were discussed, new codes were created as top-level codes to be assessed and regrouped after going through the entirety of the speech samples once. The codes were sorted and regrouped after the first round of coding and I began defining the codes that were being used most frequently. This resulted in a first draft codebook. Many of the original deductive codes were re-arranged into sub-codes, as they were not as relevant as initially thought and hadn't been applied to the texts as frequently or consistently as other codes.

3.3 Regrouping the codes and second coding process

These multiple inductive codes were then reworked into new inductive frame categories (Fig. 3) which created the main "frames" that are vaguely similar to the original 6 deductive, predetermined code categories. The original code categories were taken straight from my literature review on understanding government and health care reform. However, taking these 6 concepts directly from the literature and imposing them onto speeches and media samples oversimplifies and many of the concepts simply didn't apply. While 'rights' and 'market' stayed the same, other concepts concerning state or federal responsibility change from what had been expected. As such, the 6 overarching code categories changed into 5 categories. In addition to this, 3 separate overarching parent codes that bear no resemblance to the original deductive codes were developed to categorize purely inductive codes.

Part of the project's theory was bound up in this coding and regrouping process: The regrouping process is the process by which the public discourses and the codes can become identified as frames; thus, the coding process in MAXQDA was a major part of the theoretical element of objectively defining frames in political communication.

Fig. 3 shows how the code system looked like after modification and regrouping, with the creation of some new top-level codes that reflected the six original deductive categories, but also incorporating new codes that emerged from the first coding process (under 'Overview of inductive codes').

⌄ 🗔 **Code System**	**10282**
⌄ 🗔 Overview of 5 main parent codes	0
> 🗔 National/Federal Concern; urgency overview	757
> 🗔 Comparison with Other Nations Overview	191
> 🗔 Economic/Market Overview	3884
> 🗔 Human Rights Overview	1402
> 🗔 Democracy Overview	412
⌄ 🗔 Overview of inductive codes	0
> 🗔 What is the problem?	460
> 🗔 What is the solution?	470
> 🗔 Who is being affected? Recipients/beneficiaries/victims	964

Fig. 3:   Reworked code system with 5 main codes and additional inductive codes

In the second coding process, the datasets were recoded manually to ensure consistency. Each segment coded adhered to the codebook rules, such as each coded segment being no longer than 2 sentences in order to establish consistency. Another codebook rule stated that the parent code and sub-code must both be applied to a given segment in order for the parent code to have an overview of all sub-codes. A complete overview of every coding category that was developed can be seen in Fig. 4.

The process of coding inductively and deductively with a topic as diverse and contentious as health care reform shows how MAXQDA software allows us to challenge the predetermined categories that are often used to explain scholarly research on this topic. For this project, merely creating the code system was the first one of the important outcomes.

4   Writing memos

Following the creation of the sophisticated coding system specific to American health care reform debates, the memo function was used in coding and was also used during the whole process of analyzing the data. The memo function was used frequently to keep track of the hundreds of media samples I was coding and to identify interesting patterns. The memos are crucial in helping researchers keep track of which articles were actually useful, which ones introduced important information, and which ones were irrelevant to the research questions. Information on hundreds of news articles were succinctly summed up in the document memos. Combing the memos during the analysis was essential in uncovering patterns in reporting. Impressions about article topics were noted, including frames that had been used in speeches but were noticeably absent from the media samples. An example is how small business were coded in the speeches but were not mentioned as much in the media samples.

Fig. 4: Code system with grouped inductive codes—codes with relation to 5 main frames (left) and additional codes (right)

The document memo function was used in the form of free-written note-taking after the codes were applied to the speeches and articles. Fig. 5 shows an example of how the memo function was particularly useful when large samples were being coded and analyzed. This example is from the media samples analyzed during the Obamacare debate, highlighting certain topics to which I expressed surprise and tracking my research process. Colored memo icons were used to mark very important or noteworthy memos.

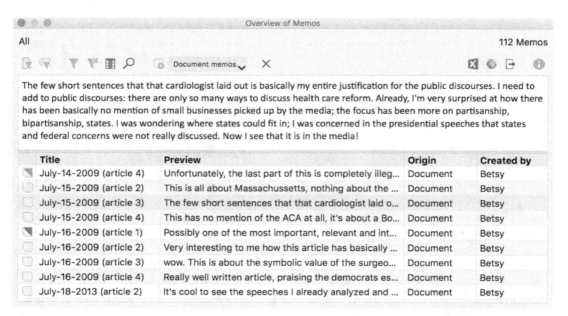

Fig. 5:   Overview of Memos with document memos

Microsoft Word was used in combination with MAXQDA, as the tabular Overview of Memos for the code memos and the Codebook (available in the **Reports** menu) were easily exported to Word for use in my dissertation. Code memos were reread and then compared with memos from other time periods in order to understand different patterns. After exporting the Codebook to Word, some minor formatting and structuring changes were integrated.

5   Code frequencies: Visualizing code usage

The Code Frequencies function (**Analysis > Code Frequencies**) was used to determine how frequently certain codes were used. This was applied to both parent codes as well as subcodes. Only parent codes are shown in Fig. 6 and 7 which are from speeches coded during the Obama juncture. The first chart "Documents with code" shows the number of documents containing one of the 5 main codes. For example, nearly all documents were coded with economic or human rights. The second Code Frequency chart "Segments with code" shows the distribution of the segments with the particular code. These charts provide important information on the dominance of the economic/market overview codes in the speeches on health care. They also illustrate that while many of the documents discussed human rights and economic frames, there was significantly more economic/market framing. The charts also show the relative unimportance frequency-wise of the three other main code categories in face of the dominance of market and rights frames.

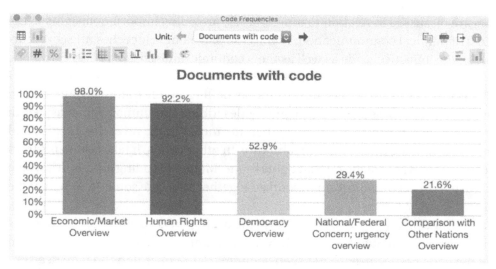

Fig. 6: Code frequencies for 5 main codes of the frame analysis (unit of analysis is document)

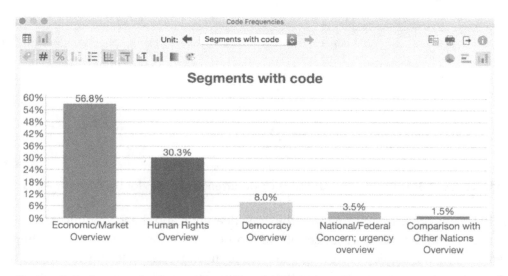

Fig. 7: Code frequencies for 5 main codes of the frame analysis (unit of analysis is segment)

6 Code Relations Browser: Visualizing code co-occurrence

One last in-depth analysis was important for understanding the interaction between codes: MAXQDA's Code Relations Browser (**Visual Tools > Code Relations Browser**) was used to visualize code co-occurrence, which is essential for uncovering nuances of frames and the presence of mixed framing techniques. Code co-occurrence illustrates which codes occur alongside which other ones. Within the scope of this project, it assists in identifying what frames are discussed in relation to other frames, providing important insights to the complex field of political communication. In the case of Obama's speeches, the co-occurrence between the 'injustice' code as well as the 'economic' and 'cost of health care' code was one area that merited further observation. Previous research demonstrated a significant uptick in Obama's usage of the "mixed" frame: neither purely framing health care in an economic or market-based sense, nor purely describing the human rights aspect of healthcare (Leimbigler & Lammert, 2016). Rather, the mixed frame revealed injustice and cost: the injustice of being priced out of health care. In other words, it takes elements from both the economic and as well the human rights frame. Manually coding for this, it became clear that injustice and economic framing worked together and were sometimes part of the same frame.

The example of Obama's speeches illustrates the overlap or co-occurrence of codes, as depicted both visually and numerically in the Code Relations Browser. The screenshots in Fig. 8 show the code co-occurrence between economic sub-codes and the injustice sub-code, which illustrates if mixed framing was occurring—and between which codes.

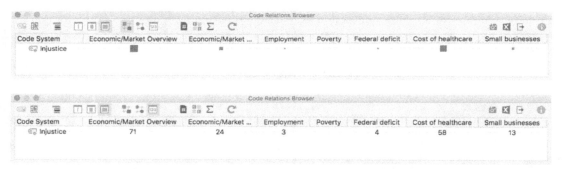

Fig. 8:   Code Relations Browser showing the code co-occurrence of codes for the frame analysis

The Code Relations Browser example with the 'injustice' code and the 'Economic/Market overview' parent code shows 71 instances of code co-occurrence, which leads to a finding that mixed framing was indeed occurring. This was particularly useful for my findings, as this interaction shows a new dimension of the data and allows for a more complex understanding of how health care is framed. This is replicable and can be used for other projects examining different types of frames and how they intersect, while continuing to build on research examining mixed frames (Leimbigler & Lammert, 2016). Therefore, part of the analysis rested upon this finding that was made possible through MAXQDA's Code Relations Browser.

7   Lessons learned

MAXQDA has multiple functions for thorough and systematic speech and media analysis. These tools facilitate our understanding of how framing is carried out. Four specific MAXQDA tools were used in this project. As outlined in this chapter, those tools included the Code System, tracking hundreds of documents using the memo functions, using charts to analyze Code Frequencies, and the Code Relations Browser to look for co-occurrences after coding all documents. MAXQDA also allowed for the easy creation of a full codebook with explanations and justification for each code.

Researchers should take note with regards to coding and being aware of subjectivity in qualitative analysis. Coding everything systematically and applying more than one code to a given segment is encouraged for researchers who want to make good use of the code co-occurrence functions, which can highlight patterns that may otherwise be overlooked. Researchers with similar datasets could replicate a similar deductive-inductive coding process. That said, caution should be taken in not creating too many coding categories, as this can easily become overwhelming.

The process of coding and re-coding will always entail a certain level of subjectivity. Throughout the lengthy process of coding and re-coding both inductively and deductively, there was often the potential of including another code or having omitted a different code. A limitation of qualitative studies is the certain level of subjectivity inherent to creating a code book based on the concepts around health care. To reduce subjectivity, only codes that clearly constituted a pattern were included. Many codes were clearly dominant, occurring hundreds of times. This means that a code used only once, twice, or very few times would not be viewed as a significant pattern. A boundary had to be drawn with regards to which public discourses and concepts became coded to demonstrate a framing process.

Another important point is the need of analyzing the relation between codes. This is significant for any mixed frames that occur, as the code statistics only show the frequency of a code being used; their interaction is not shown unless analyzing for code co-occurrence. This results in code frequency charts that may not illustrate the complete story of the data, which also points to the importance of utilizing many of the tools available in MAXQDA. An example of this is how the Obama speeches that contained a high level of mixed framing (economic and market framing together) appear with only the frequency of economic and rights framing in the charts, and no insight into their overlap, when a more accurate visualization shows them occupying the space as a mixed code, hence the importance of also illustrating code co-occurrence. In the context of this project, code co-occurrence constitutes one of the most significant aspects of coding with MAXQDA because it illustrates the mixed framing methods and which topics are discussed in connection with which other ones.

One of the most important lessons learned from using MAXQDA on a project with a large dataset is to simply begin diving into the data and coding, even when first coding processes can be messy. When faced with a new project and the ability to create an entirely new coding system, many students and researchers can hesitate and be wary of making mistakes. As such, an important takeaway is to emphasize the importance of the structure that deductive coding can provide, as well as the importance of the creativity of inductive coding. The project's results illustrate how more research should clearly highlight the inductive and deductive coding and categorizing that occurs during the coding stages. Simply diving into the data without any predetermined categories would have been overwhelming, given that over 90 codes were added and then needed to be grouped. Conversely, applying the rigid categories to this body of data without the space to add or remove major parent codes would also have resulted in missing a lot of data. Therefore, MAXQDA is essential in creating coding systems, and students in particular should be encouraged to think of the first coding process as an important initial step to create a draft of the coding system. The code-co-occurrence is also part of a major finding and lesson learned: MAXQDA affords tools that can be used to better understand qualitative analysis. Computer assisted coding can give us a much more nuanced picture of what we are researching. MAXQDA contains many useful tools for finding linkages between different codes and assisting with analysis of large qualitative datasets. Researchers looking at speeches and media samples in particular can use the simple coding and grouping functions of MAXQDA, as well as the code co-occurrence functions to gain a deeper and more sophisticated analysis of the discourses and frames in speech and media samples. This can be extended to the analysis of other types of document samples as well.

Bibliography

D'Angelo & J., Kuypers. (2010). *Doing news framing analysis: Empirical and theoretical perspectives.* Routledge.

Dorfman, L., Cheyne, A., Gottlieb, M., Mejia, P., Nixon, L., Friedman, L., & Daynard, R. (2014). Cigarettes become a dangerous product: Tobacco in the rearview mirror, 1952–1965. *American Journal of Public Health,* 104(1), 37–46. https://doi.org/10.2105/AJPH.2013.301475

Entman, R. (2004). *Projections of power: Framing news, public opinion, and U.S. foreign policy.* Chicago University Press.

Kuckartz, U. (2014). *Qualitative Text Analysis: A guide to methods, practice & using software.* Sage.

Leimbigler, B. & Lammert, C. (2016). Why health care reform now? Strategic framing and the passage of Obamacare. *Social Policy & Administration,* 50(4), 467–481. https://doi.org/10.1111/spol.12239

Proquest NYT. https://search.proquest.com/hnpnewyorktimes (data set). Data accessed through FU Berlin Primo.

The American Presidency Project. https://www.presidency.ucsb.edu/ (data set). Data accessed September–October 2017.

About the author

Betsy Leimbigler, PhD is a research associate at the John F. Kennedy Institute of the Freie Universität Berlin. She used MAXQDA to systematically analyze speeches and media samples surrounding federal health care reform in the U.S. for her doctoral dissertation. She currently researches the intersections of health policy, globalization, and power, and teaches undergraduate and Master's-level courses in political science at the Freie Universität Berlin, and policy analysis at Bard College Berlin.

Using MAXQDA's Summary Features:
Developing Social Types in Migrant Integration Studies

Aikokul Maksutova

Abstract

This chapter depicts how MAXQDA has been used in my PhD dissertation on the integration potential of labor migrants from three migrant sending countries of Central Asia. It discusses how MAXQDA supported data processing and initial data reduction, and further focuses on the use of summary functions to generate qualitative social types. The use of MAXQDA's summary function proceeds in two distinct stages, beginning with the Summary Grid and then creating Summary Tables. The Summary Grid is used to delve into the coded qualitative data and to summarize thematic highlights for individual documents by bringing the data to a higher level of abstraction. Once completed, the summarized data is clustered together to form a compilation of thematic summaries for selected document groups with a view to explore emerging patterns, similarities, and diverging trends across different research sub-groups. Subsequently, the thematic Summary Tables generated for document groups are further summarized within the theoretical framework of the study, as a result of which certain qualitative social types are crystallized.

Key MAXQDA features covered

✓ Memos
✓ Summary Grid
✓ Summary Table

1 Introduction

The research project examines the integration potential of labor migrants from three migrant sending countries of Central Asia—Kyrgyzstan, Tajikistan, and Uzbekistan—in Russia by investigating integration trajectories emerging among different migrant groups and the role of transnational involvement in these processes (Maksutova, 2019). With respect to underlying theoretical frameworks, the study applies the four-dimensional social integration model by Hartmut Esser (2001) to craft a meta-structure for data collection and analysis, and it uses transnational migration theories to examine micro-level processes taking place in and across different dimensions. Epistemologically, the study employs a qualitative hypothesis-generating approach translated into empirical research conducted in Russia's capital city of Moscow. Sixty qualitative interviews, including 48 in-depth interviews with migrants and 12 expert interviews, were conducted. The data was analyzed using the method of thematic descriptive analysis. Primary data processing and analysis were carried out using MAXQDA along the following main stages:

1. Transcribing audio-recorded interviews using MAXQDA's transcription function
2. Organizing interview transcripts into document groups by national groups and document sub-groups by interview type
3. Developing a deductive code system based on qualitative categories from the interview guidelines
4. Coding transcripts using different coding techniques (first data reduction)
5. Restructuring the code system by clustering inductive and deductive categories according to similarity, regularity and redundancy
6. Summarizing the coded interview data using MAXQDA's summary functions (second data reduction)
7. Producing category-based analytical notes and crystalizing the emerging social types

Although MAXQDA was utilized throughout the entire study, this chapter will focus on the use of MAXQDA's summary functions in formation of social types.

2   Data collection and methodological approach

I deliberately decided against applying quantitative methods due to the comparatively large size of the research population, as this would not have allowed me to reach sufficient sampling size to ensure the overall representativeness of potential research findings within the available timeframe. Instead, through the use of qualitative methods, I obtained an in-depth sense of actors' perceptions, behavioral logics and underlying motivations which ultimately helped me understand the meaning of established social regularities and uncover previously unknown relations between different factors. This was achieved through the application of a combination of several qualitative research methods, including problem-centered interviews with ordinary migrants, expert interviews with ethnic community representatives, and non-participatory observation systematized in a field journal. Interviews were conducted with the assistance of two different interview guides: one designed for interviews with ordinary migrants and a second developed for expert interviews.

While recruiting research participants, I applied different sampling methods depending on perspective interviewees' gender, legal status, employment sector, religious background, and age. For example, religious male migrants and migrants with the illegal residence status were the hardest to reach, the recruitment of whom mostly took place via recommendation of other interviewees. Concerning the interview languages, I used Kyrgyz or Russian while interviewing migrants from Kyrgyzstan, and Uzbek or Russian with migrants from Uzbekistan and Tajikistan. For qualitative data analysis, 60 interviews were transcribed word-by-word and coded line-by-line, using MAXQDA.

3   Data processing and reduction using MAXQDA

The entire research project utilized MAXQDA from the processing of interviews through data analysis. The audio-recordings of all 60 interviews were first imported to MAXQDA and transcribed using MAXQDA's transcription function and translated from Uzbek, Kyrgyz, and Russian into English.[1] The original audio-recordings and their transcripts were organized into three document groups by nationality of interviewees. According to the type of interview (in-depth interviews or expert interview), they were further split into two distinct sub-groups. To visually structure the data at a document sub-group level, interview transcripts were assigned different colors differentiating interviewees by gender. As depicted in Fig. 1, transcripts with male interviewees have a red color and those with female interviewees received a green color. All expert interview transcripts are separately grouped into a document set for easier access to the expert data. Particular attention deserves the naming of interview documents, as it can also be used for organizing and structuring data efficiently. To highlight the key identifiers, the document names included the respondent's alias, nationality, and gender. Additional information about the interviewee and the interview process, such as access to the field, interference during the interview and other research-relevant observations were documented in document memos. In addition, if a document memo used the "M" label, it indicated that the memo contained relevant excerpts from the field journal, which were linked to corresponding codes and coded segments where appropriate, to ensure that valuable observation data was also included in the analysis.

An initial deductive code system was developed reflecting the main topics of the interview guide. This was the basis for the first data reduction stage in which the cases were coded using different coding methods including deductive coding, in vivo coding, emotion coding, value coding, and initial coding (Saldaña, 2016). As a result, a unified code system was established, composed of three national categories (Fig. 1). Each national category consisted of structural, cultural, social, and identification sub-categories and a category incorporating all remaining codes.

Throughout the coding process, the code system was gradually customized by breaking down thematic sub-categories into codes, aggregating similar codes into sub-categories

---

1   The translation of the primary data from the original languages into English was necessary because the dissertation was to be written in English and not all the academic supervisors and reviewers mastered the Central Asian languages to adequately review the data in the original languages.

and clearing out redundant codes using MAXQDA's **Creative Coding** tool (available in the **Codes** menu) and other coding features. The coding was subjected to a rigorous review process which resulted in appropriate corrections to the coding system. The connotation and logic behind each higher-level code (category) and the necessary adjustments they underwent during the first data reduction stage were properly documented in code memos, so that the history of code system development could be traced.

Document System			Code System		
Documents	3083		Code System		3083
Kyrgyzstan	905		KYRGYZSTAN		0
Interviews with experts	171		STRUCTURAL DIMENSION	T	446
Kasym_Kyrgyz_male_expert	9		SOCIAL DIMENSION	T	402
Bakyt_Kyrgyz_male_expert	46		CULTURAL DIMENSION	T	61
Marcel_Kyrgyz_male_expert	44		IDENTIFICATIONAL DIMENSION	T	60
Azamat_Kyrgyz_male_expert	51		TAJIKISTAN		0
Jyldyz_Kyrgyz_female_expert	21		STRUCTURAL	T	251
Interviews with migrants	734		SOCIAL	T	507
Zubaida_Kyrgyz_female	43		CULTURAL	T	136
Zebi_Kyrgyz_female	41		IDENTIFICATIONAL	T	54
Guldar_Kyrgyz_female	42		UZBEKISTAN		0
Shukurnisa_Kyrgyz_female	56		STRUCTURAL	T	621
Feruza_Kyrgyz_female	47		SOCIAL	T	130
Anara_Kyrgyz_female	46		CULTURAL	T	66
Venera_Kyrgyz_female	72		IDENTIFICATIONAL	T	43
Uuljan_Kyrgyz_female	58		MIGRATION LEGISLATION	L	123
Umutai_Kyrgyz_female	100		MIGRATION GOALS	RQ	58
Kanybek_Kyrgyz_male	20		MOSCOW DOESN'T BELIEVE IN TEARS	!	125
Murat_Kyrgyz_male	18		Sets		0
Alisher_Kyrgyz_male	58				
Azamat_Kyrgyz_male	47				
Eliza_Kyrgyz_female	38				
Ruslan_Kyrgyz_male	48				
Meta-Summaries Kyrgyzstan	0				
Uzbekistan	1129				
Tajikistan	1049				
Sets	654				
Expert interviews	654				

Fig. 1:   Document System and Code System after coding (first data reduction)

4   Summarizing data using MAXQDA

Once the data had been coded and the coding system refined, it was time to move on to the second stage of data reduction—summarizing coded data. The summary plan (depicted in Fig. 2) consisted of four analytical steps, each of which reduces the summarized data and takes it to the next abstract level. The main task of the first analytical step was to summarize the coded documents by sub-categories, as a result of which all 60 documents across three document groups were assigned with thematic summaries. Then, in the second step, all summaries written for each sub-category were compiled into Summary Tables. For each region (document group) one table was created. In the third step, the compiled summaries were aggregated into meta-summaries, which were further exported to a text file for further analysis. In the last step, all meta-summaries assigned to specific categories across all three document groups were put together to explore emerging regularities and singularities, compare the country-based findings, and generate cross-national social types.

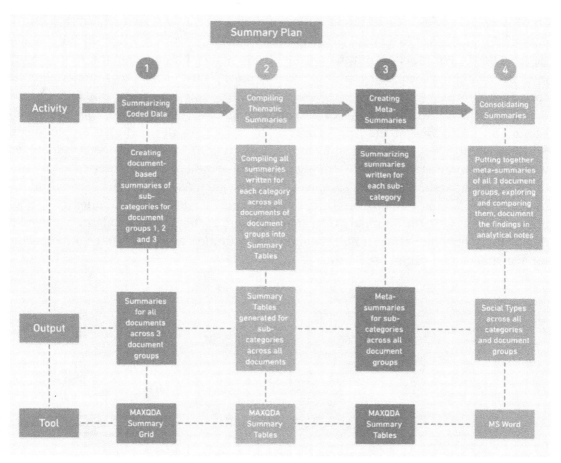

Fig. 2: "Summary Plan"

The coded data was summarized using MAXQDA's Summary Grid and Summary Table. The main idea behind the Summary Grid is to extract the key ideas from the coded segments of a topic for each document. Once written, the Summary Table compiles the final summaries for specific codes and documents together with selected document variables. Their use in the different stages of the data compilation plan will be discussed in detail in the sections below.

4.1 Summarizing coded data

To start with, I decided to limit the Summary Grid to a small portion of the dataset, so I activated the document group "Kyrgyzstan" and the highest-level code "Kyrgyzstan." Then, by using **Analysis > Summary Grid**, I opened a Summary Grid with only activated documents and codes (Fig. 3). The activated highest-level code "Kyrgyzstan" had a complex structure containing four categories of the second highest level in the code system hierarchy. These categories, which stand for the "cultural," "social," "structural," and "identification" dimensions of Esser's social integration model, were further split into sub-categories and codes. For practical purposes, I decided to write summaries on the sub-category level to encompass several lowest level codes at once. Thus, I began by summarizing the coded data from 20 Kyrgyzstani interviewees under the category "Structural Dimension" that was divided into sub-categories describing migrants' inclusion into the core socio-economic institutions of the host country. The sub-categories included employment, housing, healthcare, and legalization, among others (Fig. 3). Each document was assigned with 4–10 thematic summaries describing salient behavioral patterns, experiences, or attitudes of one interviewee vis-à-vis a specific sub-category. As a result, the "Structural Dimension" containing 446 coded segments was summarized into 103 summaries for 20 documents. In this way, the Summary Grid enabled me to examine individual interviewees in detail and to document their unique experiences, attitudes, and perceptions on a specific topic in an abstract, condensed form.

Fig. 3: Summary Grid—a summary is written (right pane) for 4 coded segments of the code "EM-PLOYMENT" (displayed in the middle pane)

When writing a summary, the edit and display options of the summary window were helpful. The options to display code comments and memos attached to coded segments in the middle column "Coded segments" right below the segments allowed me to delve into initial thoughts and insights that appeared while coding and incorporate them into my summaries. This ensured that in the second stage of data reduction no intellectual work, which was performed in the data processing and coding phase, was left behind. Additionally, when coding transcripts I often assigned a weighting score of 10 to indicate that coded segments are suitable as citations for my paper. Using the **Display origin** option in the Summary Grid which shows the weight and location of a coded segment, I could easily copy the most relevant segments over to the summary along with the source information for later use in the paper.

Having summarized the category "Structural Dimension" for the document group "Kyrgyzstan," I did the same with the other three categories "Social Dimension," "Cultural Dimension," and "Identification Dimension," and applied the same technique for the document groups "Uzbekistan" and "Tajikistan."

4.2 Compiling thematic summaries

Once all categories across 60 interviews had been summarized, it was time to move on to the next analytical step, the primary objective of which was to compile all summaries written to sub-categories within one document subgroup into a Summary Table. To accomplish this, I created a new text document in the document group "Kyrgyzstan," placed it at the end of the list, and named it "Meta-Summaries Kyrgyzstan" (Fig. 4).

This was done to have a row with empty cells at the bottom of the Summary Table for writing meta-summaries later. Then I activated the category "Structural Dimension" and the document group "Kyrgyzstan." I opened the Summary Tables tool (**Analysis > Summary Tables**), created a new table and selected all sub-categories in the category "Structural Dimension" and the variables "Migration duration," "Marital Status," "Education," "Children," and "Accompanied" to be displayed in the first column (Fig. 5). To investigate possible differences in behavioral decisions and perceptions between different social groups, it was necessary to consider the values of these variables when aggregating summaries into meta-summaries.

This resulted in a table with the list of documents from the activated document group and their variable values in the first column, followed by sub-categories with their summaries in the following columns (see Fig. 6).

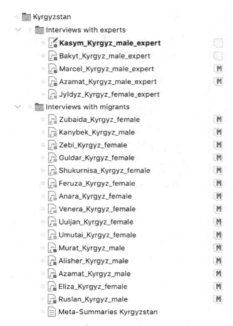

Fig. 4: Document "Meta-Summaries Kyrgyzstan" added at the end of a document group

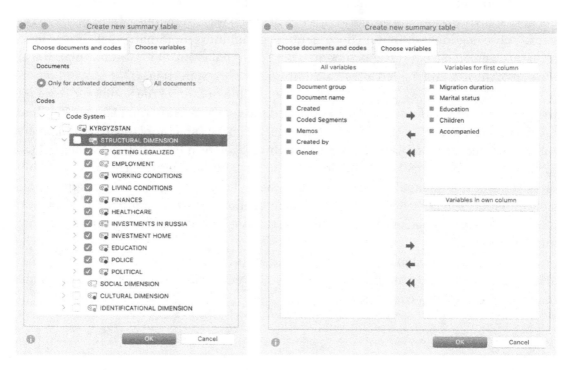

Fig. 5: Selected options for creating a new Summary Table

4.3 Creating meta-summaries

To give an insight into the process of creating meta-summaries, first, I carefully read through all the summaries written for a particular sub-category to understand the overall meaning of the summarized statements. While writing summaries entails taking the interviewees' ideas and presenting them in a concise and condensed form without interpretation, creating meta-summaries is mainly about exploring regularities, similarities, or contradictions among the summarized statement of the interviewees, and putting them into a coherent text with logical links among individual findings. This process involves the interpretation of findings by placing them in the general context of the research, comparing them with other findings, and explaining relationships. It is not always possible to explain all findings in this stage. Sometimes it is necessary to review the original research data, including the protocols from the field journal, in order to explain certain findings, or to leave them open until later, when further findings come to light.

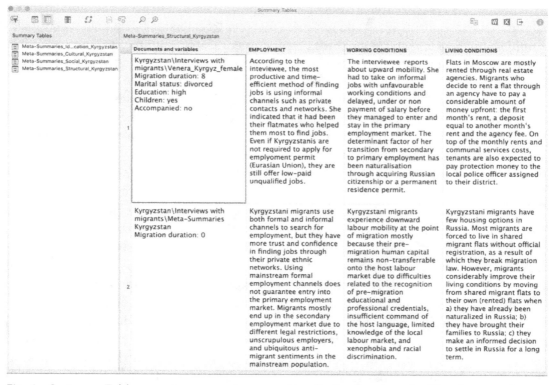

Fig. 6: Summary Tables—meta-summaries are written for 3 sub-categories "Employment," "Working conditions," and "Living conditions" in the last row of the Summary Table for the added *dummy* document "Meta-Summaries Kyrgyzstan"

Fig. 6 shows how the summaries written for sub-categories "Employment," "Working condition," and "Living condition" flow into meta-summaries displayed in the cells of the last row. These cells are assigned to the newly created document "Meta-Summaries Kyrgyzstan." To elaborate only one example of a meta-summary for sub-category "Employment," it was written based on 20 document-based summaries which were in turn produced from 56 coded segments (5,931 words). This specific meta-summary comprised 111 words. With regard to the time required for writing one meta-summary, it largely depended on the number and length of document-based summaries, and the analytical complexity of findings. On average, I spent 2–3 hours to produce one meta-summary.

4.4 Consolidating summaries

After examining the data collected within a national group, the next task was to consolidate preliminary results from all three national groups and, through comparison and further exploration, to crystallize transnational social types. To do so, I needed to export all meta-summaries to Microsoft Word and put them together by categories. The easiest way to accomplish this was to activate the three text documents "Meta-Summaries" created earlier in each document group, then create new Summary Tables by selecting all sub-categories under category "Structural Dimension," and export the newly created tables to Microsoft Word. As a result, I had all meta-summaries written to all sub-categories under the "Structural Dimension" across three document groups in a single text file (see Fig. 7). Having carefully investigated the content of each column, I added a new row at the end of the table and documented the findings in an analytical note.

The process of writing analytical notes was similar to creating meta-summaries. I carefully examined the meta-summaries from all three national groups to reveal major similarities among them, as well as divergent trends pertinent to a particular national group with regard to structural, social, cultural, and identification integration tendencies of Kyrgyzstani, Uzbekistani, and Tajikistani migrants in Moscow. I discussed these meta-findings through a lens of diverse migration and transnationalism theories, and cross-verified them with the outcome of other empirical studies on migrant integration and adaptation in Russia. In this stage of research, the analytical focus was thus on generalization, discussion, and cross verification. I wrote four analytical notes of approximately 400–600 words, one for each dimension of social integration. These notes took more time to write than meta-summaries, because the process involved not only a data reduction and generalization but also systematic cross-referencing with the rest of the dataset and existing empirical literature, as well as rigorous theoretical contextualization. On average, each analytical note took several weeks to prepare.

Once the analytical notes were written, I further evaluated them from a cross-national perspective, which resulted in developing multi-dimensional types of social integration trajectories pertinent to the Central Asian migrant population. These are empirical types induced from the analytical notes, and not ideal types in the understanding of Max Weber (1973), which constitute an artificial construction of certain aspects of reality (Kuckartz, 1991, p. 45). Social types represent the migrants categorized into certain groups based on the shared level of propensity towards social integration into receiving society. Essentially, I identified the following five general types of social integration among the Kyrgyz, Tajik, and Uzbek research sample:

I. The excluded, disillusioned and angry
II. The low-profilers
III. The adaptionists
IV. The migrant-entrepreneurs
V. The settlers

Each of these types represents a particular group of labor migrants who display similar patterns of social integration trajectories across the structural, social, cultural, and identification dimensions. The migrants allocated to each type do not share complete homogeneity in their actions, behavioral tendencies, or thinking patterns, but conform to the dominant features that categorize them into a particular group and distinguish them from other groups. Methodologically, the creation of social types was not as challenging it first seemed. The research data were subjected to a three-stage analytical generalization via summaries, meta-summaries, and analytical notes, so that social types gradually crystallized throughout the process. It remained to identify, categorize, and situate them within the theoretical framework of the research. Ultimately, I discussed the social types against the main research question and presented a number of empirically validated theoretical arguments.

Meta-Summary Table "Structural Dimension" / Kyrgyzstan, Tajikistan and Uzbekistan

Documents and Variables	EMPLOYMENT	LIVING CONDITIONS	FINANCES
Kyrgyzstan\Interviews with migrants\Meta-Summaries Kyrgyzstan	Kyrgyzstani migrants use both formal and informal channels to search for employment, but they have more trust and confidence in finding jobs through their private ethnic networks. Using mainstream formal employment channels does not guarantee entry into the primary employment market. Migrants mostly end up in the secondary employment market due to different legal restrictions, unscrupulous employers, and ubiquitous anti-migrant sentiments in the mainstream population. Migrants are not only victims of the above socio-structural circumstances, but also informed users and beneficiaries of widespread corruption schemes and legal loopholes. Thus, both mainstream employers and migrants may be interested in the sustenance of a thriving secondary employment market under the existing legal frameworks.	Kyrgyzstani migrants have few housing options in Russia. Most migrants are forced to live in shared migrant flats without official registration, as a result of which they break migration law. However, migrants considerably improve their living conditions by moving from shared migrant flats to their own (rented) flats when a) they have already been naturalized in Russia; b) they have brought their families to Russia; c) they make an informed decision to settle in Russia for a long term.	Kyrgyzstani migrants' investment behaviour positively correlates with their long-term migration plans. If migrants have the intention to return, they tend to channel their earnings to Kyrgyzstan to invest in different family projects. The migrants who intend to settle in Russia for a long time are inclined to invest in projects based in Russia. There is also a separate category of migrants (transmigrants) who invest in their home country but still plan to stay in Russia long term.
Tajikistan\Interviews with migrants\Meta-Summaries Tajikistan	[Here is another summary but omitted from the figure]	[Here is another summary but omitted from the figure]	[Here is another summary but omitted from the figure]
Uzbekistan\Interviews with migrants\Meta-Summaries Uzbekistan	[Here is another summary but omitted from the figure]	[Here is another summary but omitted from the figure]	[Here is another summary but omitted from the figure]
Analytical Note	The everyday life of Kyrgyzstani, Uzbekistani and Tajikistani migrants in Moscow is navigated through feelings of insecurity, fear of employment fraud and exploitation, and threat of police harassment, abuse and deportation. Few possibilities for legal protection and a lack of trust in the Russian law enforcement agencies and other officials have compelled Central Asian labour migrants to adopt different coping strategies. Such strategies differ from one national group to another, depending on the level of access to primary structures of the host country. Whereas all three national groups invested in their informal ethnic networks in order to address the risks and uncertainties related to their migration, some groups are already institutionalizing their ethnic structures. For example, Kyrgyzstani migrants have established a large number of migrant organisations in Moscow delivering a wide range of migration-relevant services and products to cater not only to Kyrgyzstanis but also to other Central Asian nationals. Thereby they have capitalised mainly on their citizenship, diversified social networks and good command of the Russian language. At the same time, Tajikistani migrant structures are primarily consolidated around delivering ethnic consultancy services which address Tajikistani labour migrants' pressing concerns about residence and employment legalisation, communication with law enforcement and other state agencies, employment fraud and others. Uzbekistanis prove to be the least organised and consolidated among Central Asian migrant communities in Moscow despite being the greatest in number. A comparatively low level of institutionalisation of Uzbekistani migrant structures seems to be a consequence of the Uzbek Government's hostile attitudes towards unregulated labour migration to Russia and its scepticism about the potential political role of self-organisation among Uzbekistanis abroad.

Fig. 7: Analytical notes in Microsoft Word—meta-summaries written for three sub-categories in three document groups are placed in the meta-summary table (see rows 2, 3, and 4). Analytical notes summarizing the cross-category findings are written in the last row.

5 Lessons learned

As demonstrated in my example above, MAXQDA helped me to consolidate and efficiently organize all research-relevant data in a single project. Its Summary functions not only enabled me to summarize the thematically categorized data, but also helped to conduct cross-category comparisons across different sample groups and synthesize consolidated findings from the entire research data. In retrospect, however, I realized that I had not fully exploited the software's analytical potential. After producing document-based summaries, I could have used the mixed methods analysis tool **Qualitative Themes by Quantitative Groups (Summaries)** to compare summaries for groups of documents that share the same variable values. For example, using this tool I could have cross-verified my preliminary findings on migrant women's occupational mobility across national groups by comparing summaries written on the category "Employment." In addition, I regret not having used MAXQDA's visualization tools such as MAXMaps to illustrate certain relationships and trends that were emerging in the meta-summaries. In particular, MAXMaps' Single-case Model (Summaries) would have been ideal for visually representing how the five social types gradually emerged by means of the three-stage analytical generalization. Unfortunately, I learned of these options when it was too late to integrate them into my work. So, the key takeaway for me was to thoroughly learn about the analysis options available in the QDA software before embarking on data analysis in order to take full advantage of its potential.

Bibliography

Bourdieu, P. (1986). *The forms of capital: Handbook of theory and research for the sociology of education.* Greenwood Press.

Esser, H. (2001). *Integration und ethnische Schichtung.* Arbeitspapiere – Mannheimer Zentrum für Europäische Sozialforschung 40.

Kuckartz, U. (1991). Ideal types of empirical types: The case of Max Weber's empirical research. *Bulletin de Methodologie Sociologique* (31), 44–53. https://doi.org/10.1177/075910639103200103

Maksutova, A. (2019). *Children of Post-Soviet Transnationalism. Integration Potential of Labour Migrants from Central Asia in Russia.* LIT Verlag.

Saldaña, J. (2016). *The coding manual for qualitative researchers* (3rd ed.). Sage.

Weber, M. (1973). Objectivity in social science and social policy. In M. Weber (Ed.), *Collected essays on the theory of science.* Mohr. (in German)

About the author

Aikokul Maksutova, trained as a research methodologist, works as a senior product manager at VERBI Software GmbH, the company behind MAXQDA. She holds a PhD degree in Sociology from Magdeburg University, Germany.

ACADEMIA: https://independent.academia.edu/AikokulMaksutova

Using MAXQDA for Bibliographic Documentary Analysis: Combining Automatic and Manual Procedures Within a Literature Review

Antoni Casasempere-Satorres, Marisa Vercher-Ferrándiz

Abstract

Bibliographic Documentary Analysis is an advanced type of systematic literature review that uses the research method of documentary analysis to create a data analysis process that allows us to improve the performance of literature reviews, developing them in less time or in a more accurate way. Using MAXDQA for Bibliographic Documentary Analysis is very helpful, because it offers tools to combine automatic and manual procedures within the analysis process.

In this chapter, we offer a detailed explanation of the analysis process we use in our bibliographic tasks. This analysis process is suitable for setting the research purpose, developing a conceptual framework, and even can improve the theoretical dialogue or discussion about existing research.

We introduce a project about a literature review on *financial literacy in early childhood*. Using MAXQDA, we were able to analyze 129 documents in less than a week by combination of automatic and manual procedures. Among other tools we used Lexical Search and Word Combinations to identify literature concepts. The goal was to build a conceptual framework and write an article describing the conceptual framework.

Key MAXQDA features covered

- ✓ Lexical Search
- ✓ Autocoding Search Hits
- ✓ Memos
- ✓ Word Combinations
- ✓ Paraphrasing
- ✓ Coding

1   Introduction

"In today's world, the true exercise of freedom and sovereignty is in knowledge; science is needed to lower the limits of ignorance and increase the ability to solve problems" (Ruiz Ramírez, 2010).

The significant research production of recent times and deadlines are added problems to research activity. On the one hand, a systematic review of the literature is necessary to distinguish which papers are of sufficient quality to work as a bibliography since, currently, we can lose ourselves in an ocean of information in which we find from irrelevant information to essential information (Guirao Goris, 2015). On the other hand, we require systematic processes and supporting computer tools to be efficient in reviewing and apprehending the main ideas of the texts to be analyzed in tight deadlines.

This chapter presents a case study of a systematic literature review performed with a significant number of documents. We used MAXQDA's Word Combinations and Paraphrases, among other analytic tools, to conduct a Bibliographic Documentary Analysis. The process we used was a very efficient way to explore a huge amount of literature and build a conceptual framework for future field work and data analysis and support the writing of a paper.

The analytic process was performed with 129 documents (59 reports, 35 papers, 17 book chapters, 12 web pages and 6 laws) by two members of a research team to answer the research question: *Which dimensions, aspects, and properties are discussed regarding the concept of money in a context of financial literacy in the literature that deals with early childhood?*

After the selection process for articles, books, and other documents, the mission was to review the selected literature. With a large amount of literature to review and short time frame to deliver the final report in five days, we required a strategy to optimize the work for the desired result. Conducting Bibliographic Documentary Analysis with MAXQDA provides just such a strategy and a systematic process to facilitate the necessary tasks of analyzing documents by applying documentary analysis strategies to literature documents. Using MAXQDA, we followed this sequence:

1. Formulate a one-sentence research purpose and derive important concepts from it.
2. Search for relevant literature in databases using the derived concepts as search terms.
3. Import the search hits in a reference manager, such as Mendeley, including the full-text PDF files.
4. Export the literature data in RIS format and import references together with full-texts in MAXQDA.
5. Read the abstracts of the files in order to organize the files in different document groups regarding their main topics and discard documents that do not fit exactly the research purpose.
6. Explore the literature by:
   a) Using "Lexical search" with the concept(s) created beforehand to identify relevant sections.
   b) Checking each search hit, including its context, and code and paraphrase important ones.

7. Describe the concept's attributes and properties by:

    a) Using Word Combinations function to identify additional sections in the literature, that have not been captured with lexical search but are important for the research topic and purpose in order to build the conceptual framework.

    b) Checking each search hit, including its context, and code and paraphrase important ones. Manual coding helps to develop the conceptual framework, and the paraphrases help to develop the future report or paper.

8. When reaching a sufficient degree of saturation, use "Categorize Paraphrases" to order paraphrases in the way they should be inserted in the report or paper, and the developed code system is used to elaborate the conceptual framework.

9. Bring it all together in the written literature review article. For this purpose, during steps 6–8, an additional code system reflecting the structure of the review article can be used to capture appropriate passages to support writing the review.

Step 6a and step 7a are led by word-based auto-routines; the search hits are handled and evaluated manually; some of them are auto-coded to establish thematic contexts for further exploration. The process described above is performed in three main phases in the research: state the research concern, build the conceptual framework, and perform the discussion or theoretical dialogue. In completing the literature review, the researcher should know in which of these three stages he or she is working. When using manual coding, for example, the researcher is looking for the indicators of the conceptual framework: properties or dimensions of the concept(s). The role of the conceptual framework is to drive the data collection and the analysis of the subsequent empirical study. The researcher finds the proper initial indicators within step 7. The conceptual framework is part of the coding system.

2 Data collection

This section describes the tasks we undertook to delimit the boundaries of the research by developing the research concern; to select search terms to identify literature to be included in the study; and how that literature was first brought into a reference citation software.

2.1 Delimiting the research concern

The research concern or statement of purpose is a sentence that is going to guide all the study, focusing us on the central issue and direction of the research, as Wolcott (2009) suggested, cited by Saldaña (2011). The building of this sentence provides the starting point for the literature review, in which we look at the boundaries where other authors have explored the question, and delimiting which aspects of the problem remain unexamined.

We set the following statement of purpose for our project: *Study the properties and dimensions of the concept of money in early childhood in the family and school contexts in order to build a conceptual framework to be used in further studies.*

We arranged the search system in a table organized in decreasing order according to their relevance, respecting the research concern (Tab. 1).

Tab. 1. Building the search system from the statement of purpose

Research concern underlining the key concepts: "Study the concept of <u>money</u> and its <u>dimensions</u> in <u>early childhood</u> in the <u>family</u> and <u>school</u> contexts".

Relevance	Concept 1	Concept 2	Concept 3
high relevance	money *(saving, budget, pocket money…)*	early childhood	family/school
medium relevance	money *(saving, budget, pocket money…)*	early childhood	
low relevance	money *(saving, budget, pocket money…)*		
low relevance	childhood		

After searching the combined concepts (*money + early childhood + family/school*), for example, we started retrieving results in the form of articles or books, usually in PDF format. We searched for the full-text documents and saved them in a computer folder changing their name: author(s) surname, publication year in brackets, first words of the title.

2.2 Importing and organizing the data in the reference manager

If the search system based in the concepts has been successful, we can filter the papers by their relevance concerning the statement of purpose and start adding their information fields to a reference manager like Mendeley or Zotero if we consider they will be useful in future stages of the process (Fig. 1). We can automatically import the Mendeley metadata from internet libraries or databases in most retrieve contexts.

The Mendeley folder for the project started to grow with the papers retrieved in the internet searches, and we began to revise the references in Mendeley trying to correct usual mistakes and matching APA style information for further writing of the paper. The abstracts of the papers are essential but also the full-text documents. We had to evaluate the literature quality, both in the formal aspect of the paper and the academic background of the author(s).

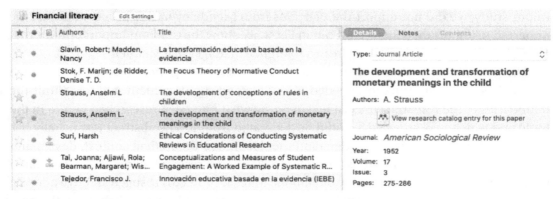

Fig. 1:   References on financial literacy in the reference manager Mendeley

3   Importing references and full-text data into MAXQDA

We created a new project in MAXQDA (**Home > New Project**) using the research topic as filename: *Financial literacy in early childhood*. We selected the references in the folder in Mendeley and saved them in RIS format (Research Information System) and imported the references in RIS format to MAXQDA to use them as suggested in the literature. The import process of the references in Mendeley is started in MAXQDA via **Import > Reference Manager Data > Import from Mendeley**.

Fig. 2 shows the dialogue box that allowed us to import the references from Mendeley and store them along with the PDF documents.

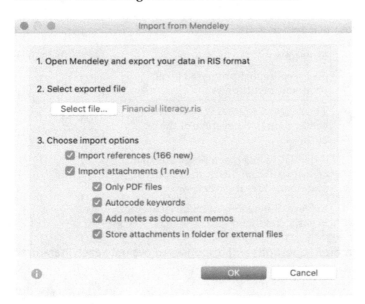

Fig. 2:   MAXQDA options for importing references from a reference manager

In our study, we did not import the PDF files from Mendeley in this process because we preferred to import them manually, but in Fig. 2, we show the different import options that MAXQDA allows when importing from a reference manager like Mendeley.

The goal was to evaluate the imported references reading their abstract field, which usually has all the information needed to understand the document and to delimit the boundaries of the research concern by analyzing what had been researched before in the topic and which new knowledge could be generated from it. The abstract text usually has all the information needed to understand the document: theoretical context, design and methods, and results of the study. In order to clarify the research concern, we evaluated the documents abstracts in the way Smallbone and Quinton (2011) suggested. We added a document memo to each evaluated RIS metadata document by right-clicking on the document's name in the Document System window and selecting **Memo.** In the memo, we can insert a layout as a table, right-click in the writing area and select **Insert table.** The table included two columns, one for the evaluative questions and another column for the responses. Questions included, which is the purpose of reading the material, the type of literature, the audience of the document, or the analytic approach, were pertinent to appraise the document. Fig. 3 shows a document memo with a fragment of the evaluation table based on the proposal by Smallbone and Quinton (2011).

Document memo: Educación financiera INFANTIL\Credit Union National Association (2009) -Report-full-draft

⚙ Type:

Calibri ▾ 11 ▾ B *I* U̶ S̶ A̶▾

Credit Union National Association (2009) -Report-full-draft

Questions	Responses
What type of literature is this?	Technical report promoted by an economic institution
How extensive are the range of sources?	The range of sources is wide but centered in the literature of the authors
Approach and methods?	A deductive approach that leads to a conceptual framework after doing a systematic literature review
Which is the central topic dealt with in the document?	Explore dimensions of financial literacy in early childhood

Fig. 3: Document memo with standardized questions and responses to evaluate each literature source

The selection of the documents began with the criteria of the dimensions of the concepts related with the research concern and the emerging conceptual framework (*money: saving, budget, etc.*), and we created document groups to classify documents by ideas and themes, right-click button with the mouse in **Documents** structure, **New Document Group**, to store the PDF files previously retrieved from the journals or databases. We dragged the files from the computer folder and dropped them to the desired document group depending on its central topic, as was stated in its document memo (Fig. 3). For example, if we found in the literature a transversal dimension with gender issues concerning *money* and *girls*, we created a document group 'Girls and Financial Education' to group all related documents. Other transversal dimensions in the project were *behavioral finances* and *education research-based in evidence.*

- Children's Financial Education
- Bloom's Taxonomy
- CNMV and Bank of Spain
- OECD
- Psychological aspects of financial literacy
- Girls and Financial Education
- Savings
- Methodology Phase II (includes evidence)
- America
- Money and Childhood
- Regulations and Legislation
- News
- Price
- Child & Youth Finance International
- Living in Society Economy
- Miscellaneous Bibliography

This initial literature review process helped to delimit the statement of purpose and to establish clear boundaries in what was investigated regarding the proposed phenomena and from which point we can go on generating knowledge. The handling of the documents from Mendeley to MAXQDA, writing the asset document memos and the study of the summary of the documents helped us to discard documents that did not fit the precise boundaries of the research concern or even propitiate the change of the statement of purpose, for example, if that topic has been widely researched in the academic community.

From the initial concepts inside the research concern (*money, savings, early childhood, family/school, …*), we followed with the task of developing the indicators to build the conceptual framework.

4   Lexical Searches: Identify important sections in the literature

The terms used in the lexical searches were found in the documents keywords or related to the concepts inherent to the statement of purpose *(money & childhood)*. Another option to find adequate search terms would be to use Word Frequencies (**MAXDictio > Word Frequencies**) to generate a list of the most frequent terms that appear in a document. Searching the literature keywords (**Analysis > Lexical search**) helped to delimit interesting contexts where the authors develop the concepts (e.g., *money, pocket money*) in their works. We usually used two or more search strings, so using the AND operator within one sentence was the proper configuration for this dialogue box to retrieve both search strings inside a sentence (Fig. 4).

The documents were organized in document groups regarding their main topic, so we activated only one group of documents at a time and performed the Lexical Search on each document group individually to optimize the performance of the analysis, as working with many documents at once might slow it down. In any conceptual framework, there are several conceptual flows, so the search strings must be changed from a document group to the other document group. It could be useful to save a set of search strings for further analysis by saving them in the Lexical Search pane by clicking the **Save** button. This way, the search strings setting is saved in the computer with the file format *.sea. Opening this file in the same pane will load the configuration in the future.

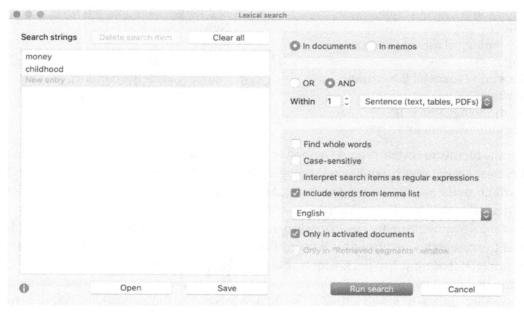

Fig. 4:   Settings for Lexical Search in the documents of a document group

Fig. 5 shows the retrieved context in the Search Results window; we performed searches and read the original text in their contexts. This close contact with the data allowed us to code the literature documents (right-click on the selection **Code > With New Code**, see section 4.1) and write first paraphrases (**Analysis > Paraphrase**, highlight a passage and start writing the paraphrase, see section 4.2).

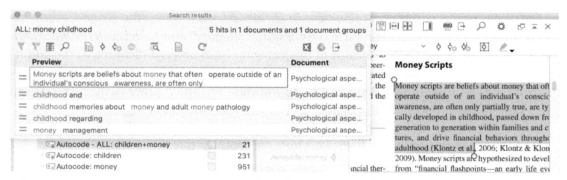

Fig. 5:   Search results window (left) and context of the search hit in the Document Browser (right)

4.1 Coding relevant sections and building the conceptual framework

In the Search results pane, there are two icons to easily code the results with an existing code or with a new one: ⬦ ⬦○. If we are exploring the documents in an early stage, we still do not know the main dimensions of the concepts from our research concern that are the structure of the future conceptual framework. Then, we use the **Autocode search results with a new code** function to code the parts of the documents with a general meaning in our project: *money* or *saving*, for example. This process is about quoting areas of the documents in which the authors talk about *money*, which is interesting, but we do not know still the direction of the narrative. We will go to these passages further on to manually code the segments with the dimensions or attributes of the concepts that are part of our growing conceptual framework. In the *money* example, we could add a dimension or subtheme, namely *handling of money*, in a *basic* way because we are talking about early childhood.

In a later stage, we used already existing codes of the Code System to auto-code the hits in the searched documents because our number of codes with attributes or dimensions of the concept was increasing (*money*, for example). In this later stage, we were building the dimensions of the conceptual framework: *money & banks, banks & savings*, etc.

In Tab. 2, we show an excerpt of the conceptual framework as a table to illustrate how we built the concepts from the coding process. The table was part of the final literature review article. We added numbers to the indicators or categories[1] to know better to which theoretical flow they belong. We have one of the main concepts in which the research evolves derived from the Spanish law related to Early Childhood Law (Real Decreto

---

1   Please note that "indicator" is a term used in conceptual frameworks that we understand as a code in MAXQDA, so you can think code and indicator are synonymous. Indicator is the proper word when talking about conceptual frameworks and code is the proper word when talking in a MAXQDA context.

1630/2006, 2007): *1. Social development in childhood*; we inserted the second subtheme *1.2 Explore the social environment* in the column "Category" and *1.2.6 Learn the basic handling of money* is the sixth indicator of this category from seven indicators. In the coding process, we found three sources of proper information about this subtopic (column "Description"), and we linked them to the appropriate cognitive process that would help teachers in the future to develop learning activities with boys and girls.

Tab. 2: Excerpt of the conceptual framework from the final literature review article

Concept	Category	Indicator	Description	Cognitive processes
1. Social development in childhood	1.2 Explore the social environment	1.2.6 Learn the basic handling of money	Knows how to count the money, buy an item, and count the change he/she might receive (UNICEF, 2013).	Identify monetary amounts with which he/she buys and receives the change
			Money can only be spent once, after buying something a person needs more money to buy something else (Jump$tart, 2017).	Explain how money can be spent once and summarize the importance of renewing it
			Understand that money can be exchanged for goods or services and that if it is spent, it cannot be spent again (OECD, 2017).	Reports that the money is exchanged for things or services and cannot be spent again

As we are doing a literature review, there is a gap between the indicator and the content of the descriptions shown in Tab. 2. We could add an additional analytic level that would include *money is spent only once* or *personal money versus others money*, but we thought this way was enough because the conceptual framework is flexible and open. It has to help us but not tie our hands, it evolves during the research process and is contrasted again at the end of the research during the discussion. The relevance of a quote in a document is decided in several ways. For example, in any topic, there are only a bunch of experts. In our project, we found good information from JumpStart, OECD, and UNICEF, or when doing a literature review on grounded theory, probably we only find three or four primary sources.

Fig. 6 shows a sample of the code system in MAXQDA with indicators for "Trust and handling transactions". In the context of the literature review, a code is a word or set of words that requires an explanation to be understood; this explanation is the paraphrase. We use the paraphrases also to build code descriptions for the indicators of the conceptual framework.

The researcher creates codes to build the conceptual framework or to support the literature review process by collecting similar ideas under one code. The researcher creates paraphrases to support the writing of the final article and to understand the codes and their future use during the data analysis. We do both actions at the same time in most cases. In our opinion, codes are proper to get indicators for the conceptual framework because, in the future, they will be used as deductive codes. Paraphrases are a fine tool for supporting the final report writing process in the field of literature reviews.

◢ ⊚ Trust and handling transactions	0
◢ ⊚ Use of money: Spend, save and share	2
⊚ Understanding of private, others and public property	3
⊚ Understand the difference between spending/saving/debt/exchange	2
⊚ Money is only spent once	2
⊚ Money and help	3
⊚ Money and saving	4

Fig. 6:   Part of the code system with indicators of the conceptual framework

4.2 Paraphrasing relevant sections to support building of the conceptual framework

"A paraphrase restates another's idea (or your own previously published idea) in your own words. Paraphrasing allows you to summarize and synthesize information from one or more sources, focus on significant information, and compare and contrast relevant details" (American Psychological Association, 2020).

Paraphrases are a way to summarize data and build analytical categories (Kuckartz & Rädiker, 2019). Although paraphrases do not require the previous coding of the data, the process contributes to generating analytical categories inductively (Kuckartz, 2014). We used the paraphrases (**Analysis > Paraphrase**) in the context of the Bibliographical Documentary Analysis as the central axis of the systematic review of bibliographical documentation and support to the generation of the conceptual framework, for example by being part of the code descriptions. The role of the conceptual framework is to drive the future data collection and the analysis, so the code descriptions must be as accurate as possible and include all the nuances of the codes, as seen in Tab. 2 example. Furthermore, the paraphrases properly organized, helped us to write the final report and the final journal manuscript.

When we found an interesting idea using Lexical Search, we minimized the Search Results window and focused our attention on the text. Fig. 7 shows how an interesting excerpt of a book chapter has been paraphrased and coded in this step. For coding, we used both an instrumental article structure code that relates to the part of our article (see section 9) in which we will include the idea and an analytic code that captures the meaning of the quote.

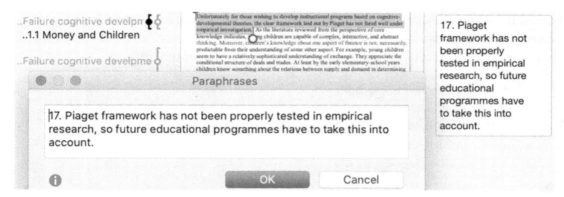

Fig. 7: Capturing an idea from the literature by paraphrasing it

After coding and paraphrasing one text segment, we returned to the search results and kept on exploring the rest of the hits. The code system kept on growing and the set of paraphrases too, our insight into the theoretical flows in the readings was wider from moment to moment. Coding and paraphrasing relevant text segments helped us to further develop the indicators, properties, and dimensions of our conceptual framework.

5   Using memos for keeping track of the analysis

Memos were also used to note the important ideas that, in most cases, relate the paraphrasing with the coding of the texts. Memos and codes are containers of ideas, in the first case there is more space to develop the narrative explaining why an idea is important in the literature review, in the second case, code names express an idea more shortly and collect segments that are related to the idea.

We used code memos to add descriptions of the codes and important information for the analysis that could be easily connected with paraphrases in the Categorize Paraphrases pane of MAXQDA (**Analysis > Paraphrase > Categorize Paraphrases**, see section 8). Document memos were used as an evaluative resource as mentioned; we inserted tables in the document memos to evaluate the documents. At the root document level, we inserted a memo with a RQ icon as logbook to write down all the important steps or ideas of the analytic process inserting the date before each annotation to keep track of the temporal flow of the task.

6   Word Combinations: Data-driven searches to identify more relevant sections

Keywords from the literature did not cover all the ideas and dimensions of the concepts relevant to the conceptual framework. So, the Lexical Search and the auto-code process only gave us a partial view. Thus, we decided to use the Word Combinations tool (**MAXDictio > Word Combinations**) to retrieve more attributes and properties of the conceptual framework indicators and categories. Fig. 8 shows the Word Combinations dialogue box and the settings we used.

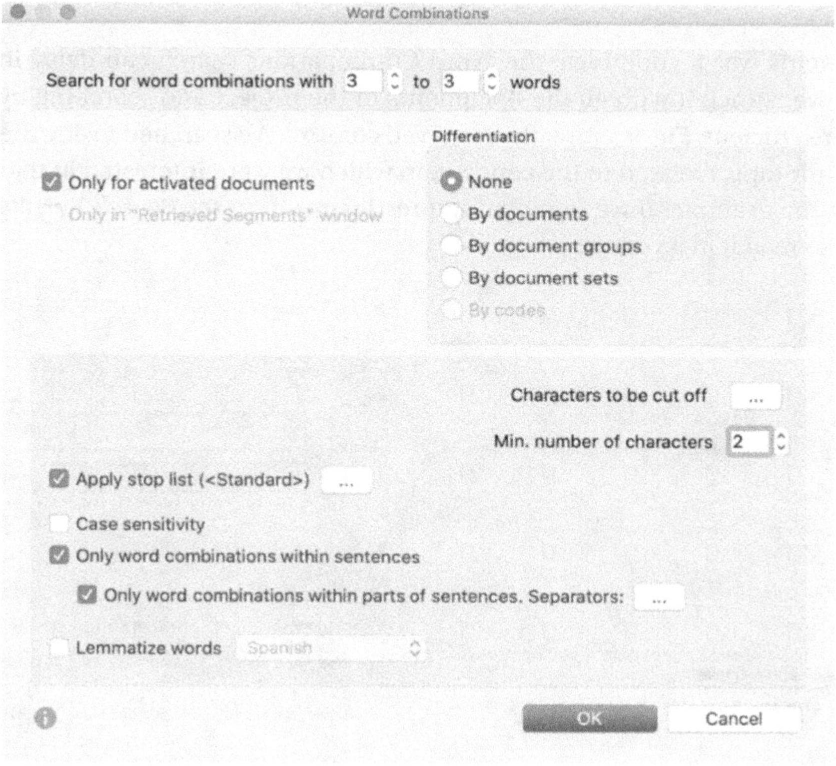

Fig. 8:   Word Combinations dialogue box

The justification of the options selection is listed below:

❖ We used to set the combinations with at least three to three words because combinations of two-to-two words retrieve much information and intuitively we thought that an interesting combination of words should have an article or preposition, a noun, and an adjective.

❖ Setting the option for **Only for activated documents**, allowed us to explore document group by document group, for example for different subthemes of the conceptual framework developed so far: *children attitudes towards money, the family role* or *the school task in training skills like saving.* Document groups serve to organize the documents by themes coming from the literature; the code system organizes the codes by themes and subthemes of the conceptual framework.

❖ In this step, we did not differentiate by documents inside the document group.
❖ Selecting **Only word combinations within sentences** or **Only word combinations within parts of sentences** narrowed the results but offered them with more quality.
❖ We decided not to **lemmatize words** in English because otherwise, the results would not be as precise as wished.

Grouping the documents was a good idea; the Word Combinations search can delay in getting the results if we launch it with all the documents in the project and searching by ideas or topics is more efficient. Fig. 9 shows the retrieved context. We searched inside the Word Combinations for topics related to the concept, in which we were interested in that moment, "biases" in the example. If we found an interesting result in the Search Results pane, we proceeded to read it in its context.

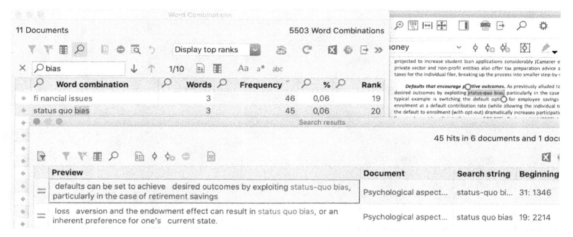

Fig. 9: Results window with word combinations (top left), detailed hits in the Search Results window after double-clicking on a word combination (bottom) and full context in the Document Browser window (top right)

In most cases, reading the quote in its context is enough to get an idea of the content and the properties or dimensions involved in that idea. From time to time, we read the full chapter or section of the document. The reason was that sometimes it is easy to find interesting ideas linked to the search hit that took us there.

If MAXQDA is provided with the right search terms, the system will do the rest. Once we found an interesting passage and read it carefully, we started working in the analysis manually without quitting the process started by Word Combinations; this is important. If the results window from Word Combinations has been closed to code the text manually, you should start the process again. The point is to take advantage of an automatic tool as Word Combinations, even searching inside the results list, and in another screen read the context of the Search Results by navigating the list of hits. If you read something interesting for the concept you are working on, you can code it and/or paraphrase it.

7 Distributing paraphrases to the sections of the final review article

The Categorize Paraphrases function (**Analysis > Paraphrases > Categorize Paraphrases**) was used to get a general overview of the ideas that were going to be the conceptual parts of our final article (Fig. 10). The table offers an interesting workspace in which we were able to have at a glance the code system and the paraphrases that we had been developing from the original texts.

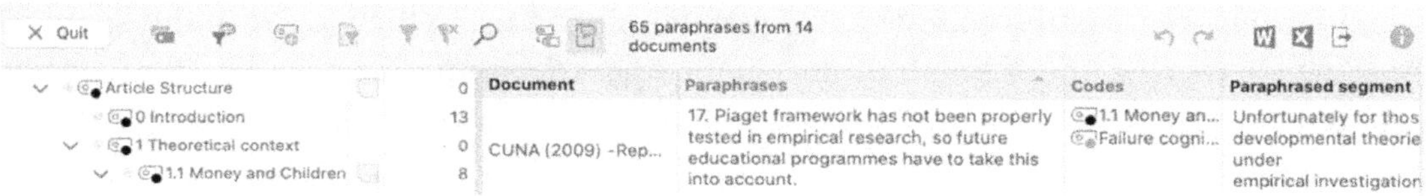

Fig. 10: Using Categorize Paraphrases to support writing the final report

We revised the conceptual codes applied to the paraphrases to know better the links between the conceptual framework and the emerging narrative of the final report or future article. We recoded the paraphrases with instrumental codes, that followed the structure of the article (as can be seen in Fig. 10), to match the ideas in our minds with the narrative of the report. During this process, we started numbering the paraphrases inside a section of the report with the logic of the narrative of the report. For example, the introduction of an article is a hard piece of text to develop, so we ordered the proper paraphrases to get a logical narrative sense.

We numbered the paraphrases in the sequence in which they will be included in the literature review article; by using this collection of excerpts, we kept on coding and working in the properties and dimensions of the conceptual framework. By the end of the process, we were ready to start writing the final report of the conceptual framework and the article. After clicking in the "Paraphrases" heading of the column to order the paraphrases by number, we exported the output into a Microsoft Excel file by using the Excel export icon. This Excel file has a beautiful landscape what we have done; we could see the source document, the original paraphrased text at the left, but at the right part we had the ordered paraphrases along with the exact part of the article in which they should be inserted represented by the instrumental codes of the article structure. The analytic codes that represent the parts of the developed conceptual framework also came along in that column to help better to develop the narrative of the article and link it with the tables inserted in it representing the parts of the conceptual framework.

8   Comparing and linking paraphrases to look for relations between the identified concepts

To better perform the discussion of the article or theoretical dialogue, we used the Paraphrases Matrix (**Analysis > Paraphrases > Paraphrases Matrix**) to compare ideas paraphrased in the documents. Comparing is useful when contrasting the same idea from different authors. For example, we found three statements that had a similar meaning but with slight differences: UNICEF states that children have to understand how money is used in the community, JumpStart states that children understand that people pay for goods and services in different ways and OECD states that children should be aware of different payment options. We examined the three similar ideas by comparing the paraphrases for the text segments and derived the code "1.2.2 Understanding in using the money in the community" which was included as an indicator in the final conceptual framework. Alternatively, different ideas that have a theoretical connection inside one (or many authors) can be contrasted in the Paraphrases Matrix.

When we found an interesting pair of ideas in two documents, we linked them. The process was as follows; first, we activated the desired documents, books or papers, for the example shown in Tab. 2, we activated the document group *Exploring the social environment* with three different documents and then used the Paraphrases Matrix to compare their paraphrases. A click on the links with the source information below each paraphrase took us to the data, we minimized the Paraphrases Matrix and created an internal link by right-clicking with the mouse on the selected text in the Document Browser window and selecting **Insert Internal Link (Anchor/Target)** in the context menu. After creating the link, we returned to the Paraphrases Matrix windows and continued with analyzing the paraphrases looking for relations in the ideas from different parts of the database (Fig. 11).

At the end of the process, we exported the Categorize Paraphrases view to Microsoft Excel with a click on the Excel icon in the top right corner of the window, as mentioned above. This way, we also exported the tabular Overview of Links window that opens with a right-click on Documents root and selecting **Links** from the context menu or alternatively choosing **Reports > Overview of Links**. With these two documents, we wrote the discussion part of the literature review article in a short period.

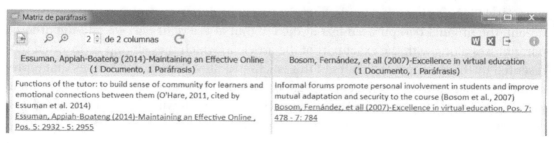

Fig. 11: Comparing paraphrases

9   Adding a code system with instrumental codes for structuring the final literature review article

In addition to the conceptual codes, we built a top-level code section labelled "Article Structure." It contained several instrumental sub-codes, like "Introduction," "Theoretical context," "Method," etc. that represented the structure of our final literature review article. Fig. 12 shows, how the code "Theoretical context" was divided into several aspects using additional sub-codes. These instrumental codes match with the main parts of the future article. This code system quote parts of the textual corpus intersected or co-occurring with the analytic codes used in the conceptual framework. We used this code structure during the whole process of analysis.

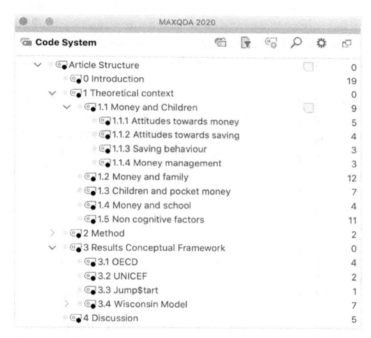

Fig. 12: Codes representing the structure of the literature review article to be written

Developing such a code system representing the structure of the final report is also very useful in other academic tasks like doctoral dissertations, research projects or writing an article. We developed this structure from the beginning but sometimes it is better to have been working with the indicators of the conceptual framework for some time because you will know better the themes and subthemes that will guide the sections of the report. This makes it easy to add the sections of the future academic product.

10 Lessons learned

We learned in this process that MAXQDA has many tools that properly combined can offer usages different from those that we initially think that they were created for. Writing paraphrases made sense in our task applied to our Bibliographical Documentary Analysis combined with the interesting lexical tools as Word Combinations in **MAXDictio** menu.

Being able to perform a quick analysis starting from automatic tools, Lexical Search or Word Combinations, combined with the manual analysis by coding and paraphrasing, saved us many hours of tedious work just by organizing the tasks differently.

The mentioned process was systematic, and we only had to focus our attention on the ideas flow that was inside the literature documents. Furthermore, the constant contact with the original data that MAXQDA enables, facilitates that the ideas inside the conceptual framework, and the later article, were accurate and close to the interpretation that the original authors had about them. Because the proximity to the data, members of the research team or the academic community can validate that the ideas have been properly apprehended.

We had prior experience both in the usage of MAXQDA and working on the topic of the research, but we are sure other researchers can benefit from this approach to perform better systematic literature reviews. Our approach has many advantages for novice doctoral candidates; anyway, they have to improve their skills in software like MAXQDA and choose a system to perform the literature review of their dissertations. In our opinion, MAXQDA can help them to optimize their time and resources better and end successfully.

Bibliography

American Psychological Association. (2020). *Paraphrasing.* https://apastyle.apa.org/style-grammar-guidelines/citations/paraphrasing

Guirao Goris, S. J. A. (2015). Utilidad y tipos de revisión de literatura. *Ene, 9*(2). https://doi.org/10.4321/s1988-348x2015000200002

Kuckartz, U. (2014). *Qualitative text analysis: A guide to methods, practice and using software.* Sage.

Kuckartz, U., & Rädiker, S. (2019). *Analyzing qualitative data with MAXQDA. Text, audio, and video.* Springer Nature Switzerland. https://doi.org/10.1007/978-3-030-15671-8

Real Decreto 1630/2006 (2007). de 29 de diciembre, por el que se establecen las enseñanzas mínimas del segundo ciclo de Educación infantil. *Boletín Oficial del Estado, 4*(4 de enero), 474–482. https://www.boe.es/boe/dias/2007/01/04/pdfs/A00474-00482.pdf

Ruiz Ramírez, J. (2010). Importancia de la investigación. *Revista Científica, 20*(2), 125.

Saldaña, J. (2011). *Fundamentals of qualitative research.* Oxford University Press.

Smallbone, T., & Quinton, S. (2011). A three-stage framework for teaching literature reviews: A new approach. *The international journal of management education, 9*(4), 1–11.

About the authors

Antoni Casasempere-Satorres is a sociologist and has a PhD in education; he is an independent consultant and MAXQDA trainer. He has worked as a consultant in numerous research projects at a European level, both in design and in data analysis with MAXQDA.
LinkedIn: https://www.linkedin.com/in/casasempere

Marisa Vercher-Ferrándiz is a professor at the Universitat Politècnica de València in the area of finance. She has used MAXQDA in research projects on e-learning and finance education.
ORCID: https://orcid.org/0000-0002-1822-5158

Using MAXQDA in Teams and Work Groups: An Example from Institutional Evaluation and Organizational Data Analysis

Christian Schmieder, Joel Drevlow, Josset Gauley

Abstract

With the outbreak of COVID-19 across the United States in March 2020, 500+ faculty and educators at the University of Wisconsin's Division of Extension began to report weekly on how they respond to emerging community needs related to the pandemic. In this chapter we share how we designed and facilitated the team-based analysis of this large and continuously growing dataset. We illustrate how we use a variety of MAXQDA's features to develop, apply, and manage coding schemes while working in a team that operates completely remotely. We share how we structure iterative workflows amongst our six to ten analysts, and we share strategies and technical tips regarding managing and merging large team-based project files. Through outlining this team-based thematic coding process we illustrate how teams can collaboratively prepare datasets for further in-depth analyses that utilizes Subcode Statistics, code-based Document Variables and MAXQDA's retrieval tools.

Key MAXQDA features covered

- ✓ Import Documents from Excel Spreadsheet
- ✓ Memos
- ✓ Paraphrasing
- ✓ Coding
- ✓ Comments on coded segments
- ✓ Teamwork Export/Import

1 Introduction: Project overview, context, and goals

The Division of Extension at the University of Wisconsin-Madison ("Extension") is a large academic outreach organization that connects the people of Wisconsin with the University of Wisconsin System. Extension operates an office in each of Wisconsin's 72 counties and in three tribal nations; our staff consists of over 500 educators, outreach specialists and research faculty—some of them integrated in county offices, some of them working from various campuses of the University of Wisconsin System. Our main areas of educational focus areas are agriculture support; supporting communities in preserving and sustainably using Wisconsin's natural resources; positive youth development programs; mental and physical well-being with a strong focus on nutrition education and support of emergency food systems; and providing community development support across the state.

Most issues Extension is working on have intensified during the COVID-19 pandemic. As an organization, we had an immediate need to understand and communicate our central and distributed state-wide responses to COVID-19, and how our staff adapted program delivery to online channels and social distancing settings. Additionally, we needed to understand how existing local issues (such as farm sustainability or equitable access to safe and healthy food) intensified during the developing emergency.

Since the beginning of the pandemic, on a weekly basis, our educators write and update brief narratives on their work and submit them to our central Planning and Reporting Platform. Between April and July 2020, we collected and analyzed approximately 1,500 narratives, with collection and analysis ongoing as of the writing of this article. Each record includes a standardized abstract sentence, a brief outcome narrative (50–250 words),[1] as well as optional narrative information on how our colleagues expand access to educational programming to under-served audiences. Each record contains background information such as the county geographies served, the affiliated Extension Institute, and project collaborators.

Our task was to set up an analysis process that would allow us to analyze a large volume of weekly incoming data. One immediate goal was to provide regular reports on our organizations' COVID-19 response, highlighting emergent areas of educational focus. Because we use MAXQDA as an institution-wide workspace for distributed analysis of large amounts of data at Extension (Schmieder, Caldwell, & Bechtol, 2018), it was pivotal to prepare the dataset for a variety of subsequent analytic questions and methodological approaches. We needed to build a database that our own analysis team, Institute-based Extension Evaluators and other colleagues (such as Program Managers) could use to quickly execute more detailed analyses themselves.

The process we describe here (Fig. 1) is an institution-wide evaluation with the hybrid purpose of organizational learning, internal program development and streamlined stakeholder communication. However, the teamwork flows and software management framework we describe seamlessly translate to mid-scale to large-scale qualitative research projects that require distributed analysis of data—especially if data are collected and/or analyzed in several stages by several teams. In fact, our process was based upon best practices derived from the project managers' 10+ year research and research management experience utilizing various Qualitative Data Analysis Software (QDAS) packages.

---

1 Some examples can be accessed here: https://wices.knack.com/recording#writing-local-activities/

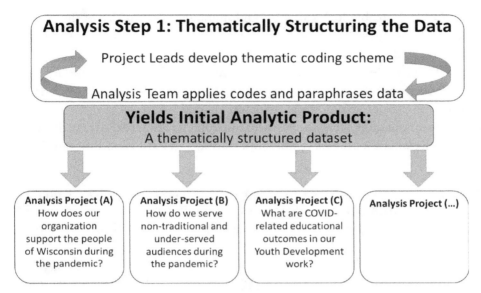

Fig. 1: Overview of the data analysis strategy for a multi-focus analysis project

2   Our approach to QDAS-based teamwork

The foundation for successful teamwork is clarity regarding analytic process. First, the team needs a clear data *management* plan: Who works with which portions of the data, and when? Second, the team needs a clear data *analysis* plan: What are the concrete tasks (Silver & Woolf, 2019; Schmieder, 2019) of analysis, and how do analysts go about them using MAXQDA? Third, the team needs a clear plan regarding the analytic *products* that the analysis produces (coding schemes, memos containing summaries, coded data, paraphrases, draft write-ups, ...). Lastly, the team requires clarity regarding how these analytic products are supposed to build onto each other and how they are represented in collaborative workspaces.

Project team roles

To develop and implement a data management plan, it is helpful to distinguish between different project roles. From a planning perspective, making explicit different project roles greatly helps making explicit the analytic procedures, collaborative workflows and expected analytic products. In this project, we had the following roles:

❖ *Project Lead.* Responsible for determining scope of analysis, deliverables and methodological/procedural design.

❖ *Project Manager.* Responsible for setting up and managing the MAXQDA file and for communicating with Analysis Team Members regarding concrete analytic tasks. In our case this role was filled by one of the Project Leads.

❖ *Analysis Team Member.* Responsible for the initial analysis of the dataset and for writing reports in collaboration with the Project Leads. In our case, the Analysis Team Members consisted of our team of Student Evaluators and the Project Leads.

❖ *Data Users.* Subsequent analysts who use the pre-coded dataset, such as Institute-affiliated Program Development & Evaluation Specialists and Extension Program Managers.

Project Managers need to be as explicit as possible when it comes to how different analytic tools are constructed based on explicit analytic tasks, combining the different components of the software and the components of other artifacts used in the analysis (Schmieder, 2019; Silver & Woolf, 2019).

In our experience as analysts and consultants it is also important to ensure that the QDAS Project Manager has enough experience as a qualitative analyst, and that the project manager has a voice at the table regarding the analytic strategy. Too often we see in research and evaluation projects that technical aspects are outsourced to team members with limited to no agency when it comes to analytic processes (such as graduate students or administrative staff). Division of labor alongside technological divides creates disconnects between how the software is concretely utilized to enact analytic processes. In turn, this is likely to foster incoherent software use, incoherent analytic strategies, and incoherent analytic products.

3   Setting up a MAXQDA project to support and structure team-based analysis

In this section, we describe how we set up and maintained our MAXQDA project file. In general, we try to put as much project information as possible into the MAXQDA file itself, so the project file becomes a one-stop-shop for process coordination, documentation, team feedback analytic products. This has two advantages: First, our analysts have all definitions and procedural updates at their fingertips, and there is no need to scrounge for meeting notes and definitions in email accounts and virtual drive folders. Second, containing all project information in the MAXQDA file allows other analysts across our organization to understand what work has been done previously, enabling to build their analysis on previous processes and analytic residue (such as coded data).

3.1 Import of data via Excel sheets

We collect the educational narratives through an online database that all 500+ colleagues in Extension can freely browse. Our data collection system exports the narratives in tables (csv files), where each record is displayed in a row. Further, every column in the spreadsheet contains the information of the different fields our colleagues are filling out when reporting. We save the files as Microsoft Excel spreadsheets and then import them into MAXQDA (**Import > Documents from Excel Spreadsheets**). MAXQDA automatically splices up the tables into single records (Fig. 2), and we can specify which fields we want to import as codable text (typically the narrative elements), and which fields we want to import as document variables (for example employee name or whether the record describes efforts to expand educational access to under-served and non-traditional audiences).

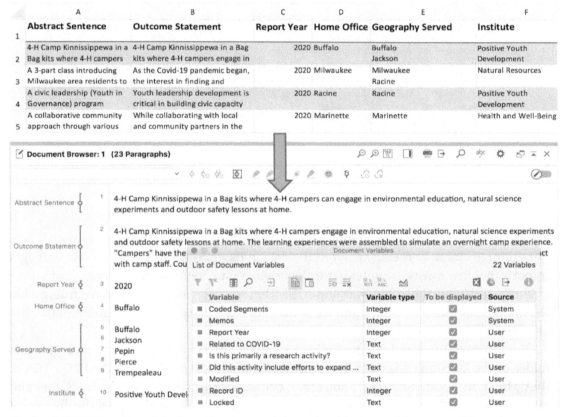

Fig. 2:   MAXQDA splices data from Excel spreadsheets (top) into codable text and Document
Variables (bottom)

3.2 Setting up and maintaining the Document System

Each time we add data, we import into a new document group (Fig. 2). This way, the data is spliced up in batches, rather than being in one large list, which makes using the team-work import and export functions of MAXQDA much easier later. We set up the document group names so they show the date range of the included data, and whether we have already done data quality control on the batch (which is the first step of our analysis). This way, our data users know the status of each batch when they do subsequent analyses.

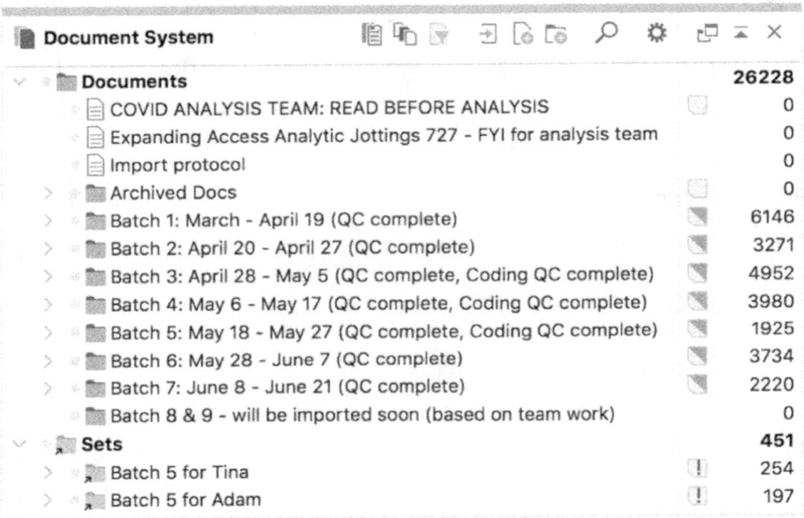

Fig. 3:	Organization of our project data in the Document System

We use the document group memos to keep track of the teamwork import for each batch. For example: Adam and Tina analyzed the data in Batch 5—so when the Project Manager imports their teamwork, he notes in the document group memo that the analysis was done by them, and when their work was imported. That way we avoid confusion regarding what the main analysis file contains, and we know who did the analysis in the different batches at a glance.

For information about the project that is important, we create documents in the root folder of the Document System. For example: The document "COVID ANALYSIS TEAM: READ BEFORE ANALYSIS" (Fig. 3 and Fig. 4) contains information about analysis roles and outlines the broad workflow. We discuss these topics in team meetings, but the document serves as a reference point and documentation of these discussions. By integrating them into the MAXQDA file, we create a one-stop-shop for analysts that does not rely on multiple shared documents.

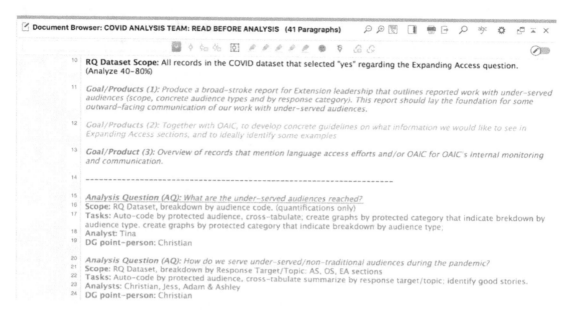

Fig. 4:   Analysis outlines and tasks are kept track of in MAXQDA in the form of documents

In our experience this helps to avoid confusion and additional communication via emails, which in turn keeps our analysis on schedule.

Additionally, we uploaded some of the resulting analytic products in a document group labelled "Archived Docs" (Fig. 3). That way, analysts could quickly reference the 'big picture' of our analysts' products, which is valuable especially if analysts work only on specific sections of the data, or if they do initial coding that is later utilized by other analysts, as done in our project.

We use document sets to create sub-batches of data for different analysts. For example, one part of Batch 5 was analyzed by Tina and another part by Adam. To facilitate this analysis, we created two document sets each containing the corresponding parts of Batch 5. That way each analyst knew exactly what they needed to work on. Using sets also allowed us to have a more controlled teamwork import process. Additionally, we used memos attached to document sets to specify details for the analysts who were assigned to the sets (such as deadlines, things to look out for, important procedural updates that may have emerged since the last team meeting).

3.3 Setting up and maintaining code memos

Memos attached to the different analytic codes contained instructions on when to use each code including anchor examples with coded text or boundary cases (Fig. 5). We also added excerpts from draft reports into the memos for the Student Evaluators in our team;

our aim was to support them in understanding the "so what" of the coding work they were doing while ensuring that they fully grasp the categories we were coding for.

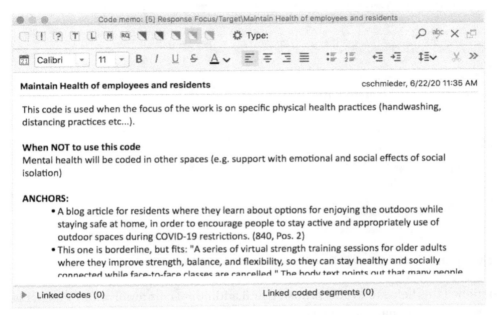

Fig. 5:   An example memo for one of our codes.

In our joint analysis sessions and check-ins, we reviewed memos to clear up ambiguities and questions, and we crafted definitions and decision guides. Throughout the analysis we encouraged all analysts to add suggestions to code definitions while they analyzed individually and in small groups. In those scenarios, we asked them to change the tag color of the memo icon to red. This way the Project Manager could easily identify where someone had made remarks. Secondly, analysts were asked to highlight their additions in the memos by changing the text color in the memo. Again, that way the Project Manager could easily see where we needed to adjust coding guides and definitions. At the time of our project, MAXQDA did not feature an option to merge memos when using the Import Teamwork function (available in the **Start > Teamwork** menu or by right-clicking in the Document System window). To mitigate this, the Project Manager reviewed memos (which was easy due to the use of colors), and then made changes manually in the core project file.

3.4 Importing MAXQDA exchange files into a core project

Our strategy related to MAXQDA project files (Fig. 6) was to maintain a core MAXQDA file into which the Project Manager imported new data and merged the analytic work of various analysts and analyst teams. We then repeated the process as new data came in through our organization's reporting system. As soon as the Project Manager merged the analysts' files into a new core file, he would archive all files into an "archived" folder in Microsoft Teams, and uploaded only the new core file. By regularly archiving files submitted by Analysis Team Members and updating a core file that would always be in the same spot in Microsoft Teams we mitigated confusion amongst the analysts regarding which file(s) to work with, and as a side effect we created a regular and traceable data backup process.

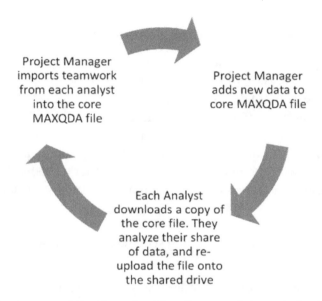

Fig. 6:   Outline of the team workflow based on simultaneous data analysis of different batches of data

To transfer the analysis work into the core MAXQDA file, the Project Manager exported the coding and paraphrases from each analyst team member's file via the Teamwork Export function. In our case, we typically export the teamwork for the most recent batch of data, which is contained in a document group (right-clicking on document group and selecting **Teamwork > Export Teamwork: Export Data to Exchange File**).

The Export Teamwork function creates a small file that contains only the coding, paraphrases and memos. The Project Manager then imports this specific analytic work into the respective uncoded document group in the core file (right-clicking on document group and selecting **Teamwork > Import Teamwork: Import Data from Exchange File**).

In general, our process for teamwork is not dependent on integrating files via teamwork import. It is possible to stagger the analysis by assigning the file to different team members at different times. We generally prefer this strategy because it makes the step of Teamwork Export and Teamwork Import superfluous. But this was only possible once the time pressure related to coding incoming data eased off, i.e., when we did not need to do simultaneous analysis to meet internal deadlines.

Regardless of the teamwork strategy, we found it crucial to communicate the merging/pushing workflow weekly with the team—that way all team members know how their work feeds into the larger process, and they understand how everyone's work and progress is dependent on each other.

4   Managing an emergent coding scheme and coding the data

In this section we describe our analytic strategy and how we used different features in MAXQDA (such as codes, paraphrases, and memos) to bring this strategy to life. Based on this, we will describe in more detail how we set up and leveraged MAXQDA to distribute this analytic process across different team members.

As a first analysis step, we needed to structure the data based on thematic codes that were relevant to our institutional response to the COVID-19 pandemic. Consequently, the overall process aligns with thematic analysis (Braun & Clarke, 2006; Guest, MacQueen, & Namey, 2012), a generic data analysis workflow aimed at structuring data around thematic clusters.

Project leads establish a preliminary coding scheme and define analysis tasks for the team

The creation and iteration of our thematic code system began with the Project Leads examining the first batch of data collected from Extension's reporting platform. Our goal was to become familiar with the data to create a rough framework that had the capacity to do some initial coding but held the flexibility to adapt as codes began to emerge. As a whole team, we later modified/re-iterated the coding scheme as we analyzed additional incoming data.

Our coding scheme was framed by the general questions we had of the data. For example, we wanted to understand what types of programming we delivered during the COVID outbreak (consulting, virtual classes, online fact sheets, etc.), and we needed to understand which broad issues (economic, health-related, etc.) our colleagues addressed in their daily work.

In the early stages of our projects, we typically utilize code comments and paraphrases, rather than relying solely on the "codes" in MAXQDA. For example, we wanted to understand how the delivery of educational programming changed due to the pandemic. We created a code "Response Medium" to represent this analytic perspective. We then applied this code to data segments that discussed the response medium. But rather than creating sub-codes right away, we coded the data via the comment function for coded segments. For example, as Fig. 7 demonstrates, we created a code comment that said, "virtual training." The advantage of this strategy is that we did not need to create and define sub-codes upfront, which could easily create a deluge of codes and a fragmentation of data. Instead, the Project Leads created code comments during the first exploration and rough organization of the data. It is important to emphasize that these code 'comments' are methodologically speaking codes—for a comparison, see for example Charmaz' (2006, p. 44) examples regarding the initial coding.

> Response Medium | 1 | A series of virtual strength training sessions for older adults where they improve strength, balance, and flexibility, so they can stay healthy and socially connected while face-to-face classes are cancelled. | virtual training

Fig. 7: Comment on a segment that has been coded with "Response Medium"

By pulling up coded segments with their respective comments in the Retrieved Segments window, the Project Leads then began sorting the comments to identify thematic clusters. Through this, they developed more stable sets of thematic categories which were added as codes to the MAXQDA project. Simultaneously, they began writing out definitions for these codes, which they stored in code memos. To test the emergent code definitions, the Team Leads then applied these new codes to additional data and modified where needed. The initial codes were now ready to be further tested, re-iterated and defined in an analysis session that included all team members (we will describe this second set below).

Some codes in our coding scheme were straightforward, such as codes that categorized different response media (newsletters, online coaching, etc.). But the Project Leads' initial analysis indicated that our team needed to read through more data to develop an emergent coding scheme that would help us distinguish between different COVID-related issues and the respective educational responses. Instead of developing a coding scheme based on an insufficient amount of data, the Team Leads decided to charge the Analysis Team with an additional task: For each record, they were supposed to identify sections in which educators described the issue they were addressing and to synthesize that description using MAXQDA's Paraphrase function (Fig. 8).

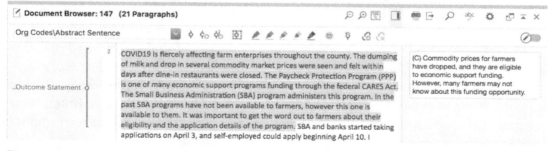

Fig. 8: A paraphrased section of data in the Document Browser

In later analysis steps (after the team members had paraphrased data), the Project Leads reviewed the paraphrases in order to establish a coding scheme based on issues and educational focus areas.

The Analysis Team collaboratively codes to establish common understanding of how to apply the initial codes and other analytic tasks

The next step was to familiarize the Analysis Team with the coding scheme and paraphrasing rules the Project Leads had created. In a virtual meeting via Microsoft Teams we provided different team members with remote control, so that they could take turns 'driving' MAXQDA. This was important because some of our Student Evaluators had not worked with MAXQDA up to that point. This strategy also ensures group engagement in virtual analysis sessions. After our first session we had established a refined workflow that included a rough coding framework with explanatory text in code memos, a realistic expectation of time demands, anchor examples to be used to demonstrate appropriate code applications, as well as a paraphrasing process.

Next, the analysis team members began coding and paraphrasing the first batch of data. Each analysis team member conducted the first coding session together with one of the Project Leads, then went on to individual analysis. Throughout the process, we met weekly to give team members space to discuss challenging records they had encountered as well as strategies they employed to make decisions about how certain records should be coded. Most helpful in these exercises was the identification of strong anchor examples for our code memos that clearly demonstrated when particular codes were most relevant. After a few weeks we decided to switch from individual coding to coding in dyads because subsequent analytic steps revealed inconsistencies in coding (see more below under "Lessons learned").

Development of a coding scheme from paraphrases and write-up of first reports

The Project Manager merged the analyzed data on a weekly basis. One of the Project Leads then reviewed the coding and conducted additional analyses. This included the aforementioned development of a thematic coding scheme based on paraphrases. To do this, he opened the tabular overview Paraphrased Segments by double-clicking on the "Paraphrased Segments" code in the Code System. The Project Lead then reviewed the list to first identify the issues and responses of each institute separately (Fig. 9). For example, he activated all records from the Agriculture Institute, using **Activate Documents by Variables** from the **Mixed Methods** menu. He could then see all paraphrases in the activated documents as a list, including the original text that was paraphrased by switching on the option **Only activated documents** (first icon in Paraphrased Segments window).

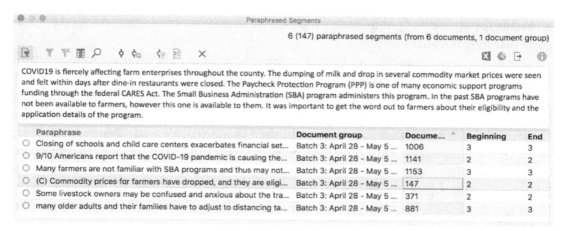

Fig. 9:   Review screen for paraphrases and paraphrased segments

In a separate document, he began to write about the different areas of issues and the connected responses. This separate document became the first report that the team shared
with leadership. The review by leadership helped us in making sure that the general analytic focus of the project was on point. Next, one of the Project Leads imported the different
Institute-focused reports back into the MAXQDA file. Based on these reports (which were
derived from the paraphrases), he developed a coding scheme (including definitions) designed to capture the broad programmatic issues and responses to the pandemic. With
this coding scheme in place, we conducted additional team analysis sessions to familiarize
the team with the codes and to further develop the code definitions, which we maintained
in code memos.

5   Cycle 3: Subsequent analysis and use of the pre-coded data

With the next batches of data, we repeated the coding process, gradually refining code
scopes and definitions. The result is a dataset that is coded based on a variety of analytic
dimensions: for example, the program audience; the program medium; the issue that is
being addressed; educational areas of focus. Through this strategy we prepared a large dataset for subsequent analysis. Our next steps consisted of focused code-based retrievals
based on whatever our own team or other analysts (such as our Institute-based Evaluation
& Program Development Specialists) wanted to learn.

For example, Institute leadership asked one of Extension's evaluators to explore several
questions including (1) What programmatic *Educational Goals/Outcomes* are being pur-
sued during the pandemic? (2) Which *Response Media* are being used to achieve those *Educational Goals*? (3) How are institute-specific *Educational Goals* associated with organizational *Response Focus Areas*? Analysis of these questions served a variety of purposes,

including the creation of public-facing reports and data summaries that were used for program planning purposes.

To complete the analysis, the Evaluator approached the data using a multi-step process. First, the program evaluator completed an initial review and cleaning of the data by retrieving coded segments for each code. Miscoded segments were re-coded as necessary. Next, the evaluator analyzed and coded all documents that had been previously coded as "unsure". This "unsure" category was established in MAXQDA's Code System during the initial coding phase to flag any data segments that were unclear to analysts so they could later be categorized by other analysts who had specific program content expertise. As a final data cleaning step, the evaluator scanned the retrieved segments for each code of interest and flagged 1–2 segments as "anchoring examples" that would later be exported to highlight specific themes.

Following the program-focused data cleaning, the evaluator relied on three MAXQDA analysis tools to create a summary report for leadership. The **Subcode Statistics** tool (available after right-click on the parent code or in the **Codes** menu) was used to describe educational approaches, audiences, issue areas, and delivery modes—answering leadership's questions such as: "What are the most common educational approaches being used by colleagues?" Next, the Crosstab feature (**Mixed Methods > Crosstab**) helped to answer more complex questions, including "Which types of educational delivery mode are being used to serve X type of program audience?" Rather than exporting tabular crosstab results, the evaluator summarized the information in text. The Interactive Quote Matrix (**Mixed Methods > Interactive Quote Matrix**) as well as a simple export of compiled text segments in the Retrieved Segments window allowed the evaluator to provide narrative examples. As an appendix to a written summary report, the evaluator also provided an export of selected coded segments for each thematic code of interest.

While the primary benefit of the pre-coded dataset was the accelerated generation of focused summary reports for leadership, it had two ancillary benefits. First, the evaluator could use the dataset to run quick analyses during program planning meetings with leadership. As an example, during one meeting, leadership asked the evaluator to quickly explain if X audience was being engaged through a type of educational programming. Because of the organization of the dataset, questions such as that could be immediately answered with Crosstabs and Subcode Statistics. Second, the summary reports and data-driven conversations illuminated gaps in the reporting and limitations of the data/reporting. Knowing those limitations, leadership identified new themes for the larger analysis team to investigate in future cycles and crafted communication to colleagues regarding reporting tips and resources.

6 Lessons learned

Giving analysts more time to co-analyze

After a few collaborative coding sessions in late March and early April, we assigned portions of the data to code and paraphrase to Analysis Team Members. The rationale for the shift to individual coding was a practical one because we wanted to provide leadership and stakeholders with timely information in a rapidly developing crisis. Additionally, our student evaluators worked on a different schedule. However, the Project Leads quickly found in that our code definitions and shared understanding was not evolved enough; to test this hunch, we also employed inter-coder reliability tests that indicated that we needed to work more closely together until our teams' understanding of the relationships between the defined codes and the data was more aligned. To counter this, we set up more frequent team analysis sessions, and we assigned the coding/paraphrasing processes to dyads of Analysis Team Members.

Reducing file sizes

Every time a colleague modified their program narratives in the reporting portal, we re-imported and re-analyzed it. That way we always looked at the newest version(s) of the rapidly changing pandemic responses our colleagues implemented. After three months' worth of reporting data we realized that the size of our MAXQDA file began to strain some of our laptops; at this point, the file has grown to over 50 MB in size. We also knew that we needed to purge duplicate outdated documents so that Subcode Statistics (**Codes > Subcode Statistics**) would be meaningful.

To purge duplicates, one of our analysis team members used **Variables > Data Editor for Document Variables** to identify duplicate document names. She then flagged the outdated duplicates in the Data Editor by changing the document color. We could then activate documents by document color (right-click on the root of the Document System window and selecting **More... > Activate Documents by Color**) and move all activated documents into an empty document group (right-click on the document group and selecting **Move Activated Documents Here**). We then made a backup of the file and deleted the document group that contained all duplicates.

Bibliography

Braun, V., & Clarke, V. (2006). Using thematic analysis in psychology. *Qualitative Research in Psychology, 3*(2), 77–101. https://doi.org/10.1191/1478088706qp063oa

Charmaz, K. (2006). *Constructing grounded theory: A practical guide through qualitative analysis.* Sage.

Guest, G., MacQueen, K., & Namey, E. E. (2012). *Applied thematic analysis.* Sage.

Schmieder, C. (2020). Qualitative data analysis software as a tool for teaching analytic practice: Towards a theoretical framework for integrating QDAS into methods pedagogy. *Qualitative Research, 20*(5), p. 684–702, https://doi.org/10.1177/1468794119891846

Schmieder, C., Caldwell, K. E. H., & Bechtol, E. (2018). Readying extension for the systematic analysis of large qualitative data sets. *Journal of Extension, 56*(6), 8.

Silver, C., & Woolf, N. (2019). Five-level QDA method. In P. Atkinson, S. Delamont, A. Cernat, J.W. Sakshaug, & R.A. Williams (Eds.), *SAGE Research Methods Foundations.* https://www.doi.org/10.4135/9781526421036818833

Acknowledgments

Special thanks go to our Student Evaluators Tina Dhariwal, Yuxin Liu, Adam Kanter, Ben Peterson, and Jess Mullen—this work would not have been possible without you!

About the authors

Christian Schmieder, PhD serves as Data Specialist and Data Governance Leader at the University of Wisconsin – Madison, Division of Extension. He has used MAXQDA since 2005 in a broad variety of research and evaluation projects and has been a MAXQDA trainer since 2009. His research focuses on qualitative methods pedagogy and the use of QDAS in qualitative analysis.
ORCID: https://orcid.org/0000-0003-1324-6141

Joel Drevlow, EdM is the Data Services Specialist at the University of Wisconsin – Madison, Division of Extension. He works with MAXQDA in various research and evaluation projects and trains colleagues to use MAXQDA to conduct their own analysis. In addition, he provides training and guidance to help colleagues generate high quality data regarding their work with Extension.

Josset Gauley, PhD is a Program Development and Evaluation Specialist at the University of Wisconsin – Madison, Division of Extension. His research focuses on youth empowerment in school and community settings. He uses MAXQDA for collaborative data analysis and evaluation of youth and community development programs.
ORCID: https://orcid.org/0000-0002-5245-9142